The Quest for the Wicker Man

History, folklore and Pagan perspectives

Edited by
**Benjamin Franks, Stephen Harper,
Jonathan Murray and Lesley Stevenson**

With contributions from
Gary Carpenter, Brigid Cherry, Robin Hardy, Anthony J. Harper,
Judith Higginbottom, Paula James, Mikel J. Koven,
Donald V. L. Macleod, Luc Racaut, Richard Sermon
and Melvyn J. Willin

Luath Press Limited

EDINBURGH

www.luath.co.uk

In affectionate memory of Anthony J. Harper

First Edition 2006

The authors' rights to be identified as authors of this book under the
Copyright, Designs and Patents Act 1988 has been asserted.

The paper used in this book is recyclable. It is made from low
chlorine pulps produced in a low energy, low emission manner
from renewable forests.

The publisher acknowledges subsidy from

Scottish **Arts** Council

towards the publication of this volume.

Printed and bound by
Creative Print and Design, Ebbw Vale

Typeset in 10.5pt Sabon

Contents

Introduction:
The search for *The Wicker Man*

**Benjamin Franks, Stephen Harper, Jonathan Murray,
Lesley Stevenson**

The Wicker Man has been a hard film to categorise: part thriller, part detective story, part horror, with not a little humour and erotic titillation thrown in for good measure. Its enduring appeal and fascination for a variety of audiences continues even after the 30th anniversary of its UK theatrical release. In 2002 Scotland's *The Sunday Mail* placed it as one of the top ten films with a Scottish theme[1] and in 2003 the film was included in the top half of Channel 4's *100 Greatest Scary Moments*.[2] In October 2004 it was placed sixth in *Total Film*'s top ten 'Greatest British films', beating the likes of *Kind Hearts and Coronets* (1949) and *Lawrence of Arabia* (1962).[3]

Its cultural impact has been significant. The creators of cult British TV comedy (now also a film) *The League of Gentlemen* (BBC2, 1999-2003; Bendelack, 2005) openly acknowledge their debt to *The Wicker Man*,[4] whilst a recent episode of the ITV comedy-drama series, *Distant Shores*, starring Peter Davidson, was given over to an extended *Wicker Man* pastiche. An incoming authority figure, a doctor from the mainland, arrives on a remote Scottish island and falls under the misconception that the locals are planning to sacrifice him by burning him alive. The episode includes the villagers gathered together at a fête wearing masks; there are many barely veiled pagan references

---

[1]   Anon, 'The Best Scottish Films Of All Time'.

[2]   Ranked 34 in Channel 4, *Greatest Scary Moments*, October 25-26, one place behind *The Sixth Sense* (1999). See Channel 4, '100 Hundred Greatest Scary moments from film, TV, advertising and pop'.

[3]   See Dent, 'Get Carter voted best British film'.

[4]   Anon, 'Gents in a league of their very own'. See too Gibb, 'A League of Their Own'.

and the local laird makes a symbolic sacrifice by the sea. It reaches its climax at a festive gathering where the physician mistakes friendly attempts to embrace him by the locals, some carrying burning torches, for a concerted effort at capture, at which the panicked 'innocent' repeats Sergeant Howie's injunction for divine intervention.

The Wicker Man's climax has developed its own totemic power, and not just in the iconography of rock groups such as Iron Maiden;[5] blazing sacrifice has also become a focal point for festivals across the Western world, including the Burning Man Festival in Nevada and the Butser Festival of Beltane in Hampshire. It has also become the highlight of the Wickerman Festival, an alternative music event held since 2002 near Kirkcudbright in South West Scotland, one of the original shooting locations for the film.[6]

This volume emerged from a cross-disciplinary conference, '*The Wicker Man*: Rituals, Readings and Reactions', held at the University of Glasgow's Crichton Campus in Dumfries on 14-15 July, 2003.[7] The event was the 'first ever academic conference'[8] about the film and attracted speakers and participants from across Britain, Canada and the United States. The location was pertinent, as Dumfries lies close to Kirkcudbright, Creetown and Burrowhead, which were amongst the film's most notable locations. The hosting institution, in addition to being part of the only Higher Education campus in the Dumfries and Galloway region, also had a range of staff from across the disciplines with a keen interest in the film.

The reaction to news that a conference was being planned on this theme was almost entirely positive. Academics from a range of specialisms – including Anthropology, Archaeology, Classical Studies, European Languages, Film Studies, History, Media Theory,

---

5   See Sermon, '*The Wicker Man*, May Day and the Reinvention of Beltane', in this volume.

6   Robin Hardy, the film's director, was an early supporter of the Wickerman Festival; see Khan and MacMillan, 'Cult of Wicker Man sets tourism on fire'.

7   For a review of the conference see Koven, 'Keeping the appointment'.

8   Ramsay, 'Actors get extra time', p. 21. See too Simpson, 'More credits roll'.

Musicology, Philosophy, Religious Studies and Tourism Studies –
offered to present papers, as did significant film practitioners:
Robin Hardy, *The Wicker Man*'s director, and Gary Carpenter, the
film's associate music director. Local residents who had been extras
three decades ago also attended and sent in mementos of their participation. There were a few less enthusiastic, but nonetheless fascinating, reactions. An anonymous poison-pen letter was sent to
the organisers, warning of dire spiritual consequences in putting on
such an event, whilst a publicity-hungry Catholic priest warned that
the conference was bringing academic 'credibility' to the 'occult'.[9]
The ability of the film to rouse religious passion and provoke debate
remains unchanged after more than three decades. Thus it was felt
to be appropriate to create a collection of papers that explored *The
Wicker Man*'s different paradigms of the sacred; that investigated the
spiritual and historical themes of the film (Christian, pre-Christian,
Pagan and heathen), and how these had been interpreted and
applied in contemporary cultural practices.

Inevitably in a collection dedicated to the exploration of *The
Wicker Man*'s historical and anthropological themes, several contributors refer to two works that are of central importance to the
film's conception of paganism: Julius Caesar's *Gallic Wars* and J.
G. Frazer's Victorian classic *The Golden Bough*. Where possible,
the editors have sought to minimize any repetition or overlap of
material relating to these sources; elsewhere, we have allowed the
contributors to explain and analyze these texts at greater length in
order to illustrate the complexity of Hardy and Shaffer's relation
to their historical material. Another caveat relates to the terminology
used in this text, particularly such contentious terms as 'Paganism',
'pagan' and 'Neo-Paganism'. The capitalised versions, 'Pagan' and
its derivatives, are used to describe an identifiable set of spiritual
practices or coherent set of beliefs concerning magic, pantheism
and the moral principles thus derived. The upper case term is applied
both to systematised pre- and non-Christian groupings from the
pre-Industrial era, as well as to the new spiritual movements that

---

[9]   Mcdonald, 'Exorcist warns of occult dangers', p. 12.

developed from the 1950s and '60s to the present. Some authors, however, prefer to use the term 'Neo-Pagan' for these post-war religious movements and this has been respected in their individual submissions. The lower case 'pagan' is mainly used to cover any unsystematised religious or mystical belief that lies outside standard monotheism. Thus, some of the cultural uses of *The Wicker Man* are Pagan as well as pagan. It is these appropriations and their historical roots that are the main themes of the collection.

The collection starts, suitably, with a contribution from *The Wicker Man*'s director and co-author, Robin Hardy, in which he discusses the motivations behind the film's creation. In particular, Hardy emphasises that the two authors (himself and Anthony Shaffer), who used as their sources the works of James Frazer and the folk song collections of Cecil Sharp, had a shared interest in the questions raised by the old religions. Hardy also draws attention to how these elements were then integrated with the themes of 'games-playing' and manipulation, which *The Wicker Man* shares with Shaffer's other works, in particular *Sleuth* (1970).

Richard Sermon's chapter, '*The Wicker Man*, May Day and the Reinvention of Beltane', introduces many of the topics developed in other contributions: in particular, the connections between motifs in the film and the historical record, and how the film's referents have been re-interpreted in more contemporary cultural productions. In Sermon's case, he examines how significant characteristics of the film relate to archaeological research into sacrificial rites and fire ceremonies, and how such rites and ceremonies have been adopted into more contemporary folk events in Europe and the Americas.

Whilst Sermon's account concentrates on Celtic, nineteenth century Celtic Revival and modern Pagan practices, Paula James' essay 'Ritualistic Behaviour in *The Wicker Man*' focuses its attention on the parallels between the film and Greco-Roman rituals structuring the preparation of human scapegoats. These include: the preliminary dressing of the victim in costume, the ceremony of the *lustrum*, in which the scapegoat is paraded around the community, and the symbolic importance of willow, which is figured in the film by the landlord's daughter of the same name and the confining material

of the burning cage. James places the film's ritual allusions in the context of their historical origins and also discusses them in relation to their more modern connotations.

By contrast, Luc Racaut's contribution, 'Sacrifice, Society and Religion in *The Wicker Man*', draws out the religious resonances and symbolic features of the film derived from the Early Modern period. Like Sermon and James, Racaut acknowledges the debt that the screenwriters, Hardy and Shaffer, pay to James Frazer's *The Golden Bough*, but it is the use of Christian symbolism that is the crux of this essay. The role of martyrdom and its ceremonial re-enactment in the Eucharist are explained to highlight Howie's traumatic, but nevertheless ambiguous, execution. Accounts of human sacrifice are a feature of French sectarian literature of the Early Modern period, and the political uses to which these accounts were put are compared to the power plays that unfold within *The Wicker Man*.

Rather than concentrate on different historical influences based broadly within the European context, Donald V. L. Macleod's contribution draws upon the similarities between *The Wicker Man* and anthropological films investigating different non-Western communities. Macleod draws comparisons between Howie's position within the film and the field anthropologist exploring non-occidental societies. Macleod also examines the parallels between the fictionally contrived action in a narrative feature film and the construction of 'real events' within anthropologic documentaries such as *Nanook of the North* (1922). Just as Howie's investigation of Summerisle uncovers his own personal conflicts and prejudices, so too do ethnographic films, which, despite their apparent scrutiny of other forms of life, end up revealing the hidden presuppositions of the researcher and film-maker's own culture.

In 'The Folklore Fallacy' Mikel Koven analyses the use of myths and legends within feature films in general, and the use of *The Golden Bough* within *The Wicker Man* more specifically. Koven suggests that there is a 'folklore fallacy' at work, in which the more the details from folklore are applied to a film to increase its veracity, the more problematic these elements become. In particular, Koven

assesses the way in which the creators of *The Wicker Man* uncritically drew upon Frazer's use of Caesar's account of the Wicker Colossus in the *Gallic Wars*, interpreting it not as a folkloristic description, but as an accurate historical source. Such constructed accounts of human sacrifice, as in the context of France's religious wars described by Racaut, served particular political purposes, and their subsequent use in fiction can reinforce or subvert much earlier value-laden messages. For Koven, the fallacy develops that, the more a culturally disparate medley of folklore elements appear in a given film in order to bolster its claims to verisimilitude, the less realistic becomes the 'authentic' combination of traditional beliefs and practices presented onscreen, as no society has, or could have, supported such a complex cross-cultural mix.

The tension between the authorial intention of making an anti-cult film and the popular reception and manipulation of the film's themes in cultish terms is the subject of Anthony J. Harper's contribution. Whilst Hardy and Shaffer wanted the audience to eventually side with traditional virtues, audiences have found alternative interpretations. Harper draws attention to the film's interplay of ideas, in particular the debates between Howie, representing orthodox Christian values, and Lord Summerisle, representing the counter-cultural paradigm. It is this play of ideas, rather than the chilling final imagery, that Harper argues is the main reason for the film's enduring appeal and the contested readings between its different audiences.

Brigid Cherry uses audience surveys to examine the way female film fans react to and appropriate the film in ways that potentially subvert authorial intentions. Cherry examines the features that particularly appeal to female audiences, such as the portrayal of female sexuality. Whilst this is a motif of many horror film classics, *The Wicker Man* challenges many of the standard features of the genre, by having the male lead represent virginity and allowing the expression of free female libidinal desire to go unpunished.

Judith Higginbottom also considers the reception of *The Wicker Man*, but focuses on it from the self-identifying Pagan perspective, which is defined and defended. Despite Hardy and Shaffer's well-documented hostility to new age practices, Pagans and Wiccans

have embraced the film, finding in it a positive representation of their rituals and beliefs. *The Wicker Man*'s portrayal of Paganism is compared favourably with that in other films; examples include works made by Pagans, such as the avant-garde cinema of Kenneth Anger, and those that endorse a tolerant approach to magical belief, such as Jacques Tourneur's *Night of the Demon* (1957).

An acknowledgement and exploration of the explicitly Pagan perspective also infuses Melvyn J. Willin's chapter, in his account of the use of music in *The Wicker Man*. Willin outlines the role which music plays in contemporary Pagan practices and rituals, and argues that the music featured in *The Wicker Man* is allied to Pagan ideals. Offering an account of the film's soundtrack, Willin's concern is to show how the music enhances the atmosphere of the film.

The influential role of *The Wicker Man*'s soundtrack is also addressed in an illuminating penultimate chapter by the film's associate music director, Gary Carpenter. Carpenter addresses the selection process, the purposes which the various components of the soundtrack play within the film, and how the recorded music has developed a cultural life of its own.

In a book concerned with Paganism, with its key themes of regeneration and renewal, it is perhaps fitting to end where we began, with *The Wicker Man* director Robin Hardy. In an interview with conference co-organiser Jonathan Murray, Hardy explains his opinions of the performances given by Edward Woodward (Sergeant Howie) and Christopher Lee (Lord Summerisle), details the problems of film-making in 1970s Britain that influenced the film's construction, describes its manipulation in the hands of the producers and distributors and outlines the work done by the film's many advocates in enabling it to reach its audience. This is followed by a question and answer session with members of the audience present at *The Wicker Man* conference.

A second, complementary selection of papers from the conference is also available. This collection concentrates broadly on theoretical analyses of the motion picture; it is titled *Constructing 'The Wicker Man': Film and Cultural Studies Perspectives* and is published by University of Glasgow Crichton Publications.

The conference, and latterly this book, were only made possible through the efforts of a large number of people, including Steven Gillespie, Dr Helen Loney, Dr Donald Macleod, Prof Rex Pyke, Frank Ryan and Prof Rex Taylor. Special mention must be made of Nick Jennings and Tina Worsey, who administrated the conference so successfully, and the invaluable assistance of Dr Belle Doyle, formerly of the South West Scotland Screen Commission, for her advice, enthusiasm and expertise in setting up the parallel film festival. We are also grateful for the encouragement offered by Robin Hardy. In addition we wish to express our appreciation to all those who attended and supported the conference for their thoughtful and passionate participation, and to those organisations who provided sponsorship and commercial assistance (Canal+, Dumfries and Galloway Council, Dunfermline Building Society, South West Scotland Screen Commission and the University of Glasgow). Our thanks also go to Gavin MacDougall of Luath for his valuable assistance with this project, and to Tim West, also of Luath, for his thorough and helpful copy editing of the manuscript.

Bibliography

Anon, 'Gents in a league of their very own', *The Gloucester Citizen*, 16 January 1999, p. 15.

Anon, 'The Best Scottish Films Of All Time', *The Sunday Mail*, 25 August 2002, p. 16.

Channel 4, '100 Hundred Greatest Scary moments from film, TV, advertising and pop', http://www.channel4.com/film/newsfeatures/microsites/s/scary/results_40-31_2.html [Accessed 2 February 2005].

100 Greatest Scary Moments (Channel 4), 25-26 October 2003.

Distant Shores (ITV), 5 January 2005.

Dent, J., 'Get Carter voted best British film', *The Guardian*, 4 October 2004, p. 6.

Gibb, E., 'A League of Their Own', *Scotland on Sunday*, 3 December 2000, p. 2.

Hamer, R. (Director), *Kind Hearts and Coronets* (Warner, 1949).

Khan, S. and A. MacMillan, 'Cult of Wicker Man sets tourism on fire: Film draws thousands to remote Scottish village for festival as remake is planned', *The Observer*, 14 July 2002, p. 12.

Koven, M., 'Keeping the appointment', in *Scope: An online journal of Film Studies*, www.nottingham.ac.uk/film/journal/conrep/confreports_augo 4.htm [Accessed 23 February 2005].

Lean, D. (Director), *Lawrence of Arabia* (Colombia Tri-Star, 1962).

Mcdonald, T., 'Exorcist warns of occult dangers', *The Sunday Mail* (Glasgow), 29 June 2003, p. 12.

Ramsay, H., 'Actors get extra time', *The Mirror*, 30 June 2003, p. 21.

Sermon, R., '*The Wicker Man*, May Day and the Reinvention of Beltane', in *The Quest for the Wicker Man*, ed. B. Franks, S. Harper, J. Murray and L. Stevenson (Edinburgh: Luath, 2005).

Simpson, C., 'More credits roll in for the Wicker Man as university makes it subject of serious debate', *The Herald* (Glasgow), 2 January 2003, p. 6.

The Genesis of *The Wicker Man*

Robin Hardy

I WAS HONOURED to be invited to '*The Wicker Man*: Rituals, Readings and Reactions' conference[10] to address a group of academics who have found so much of significance in a film we made thirty years ago, and made, I might add, with no more expectations for its reception than that it would be treated as an 'intriguing entertainment'. That it would leave its audience with food for thought was indeed a bonus for which we hoped, but we would never have dreamed to what a degree that hope would be fulfilled. I am fascinated and impressed by the scope of possible reflections, ideas and reactions that have come out of this film.

I propose here to tell of the thought processes that brought my friend and business partner, Anthony Shaffer (Tony), and I to create the film the way it is, the main virtue of which was its originality. This, however, was also its main fault as far as the film distributors were concerned. It is fair to agree with Mike Deeley, successor to Peter Snell as CEO of British Lion, who in my opinion butchered the film and did everything to destroy or delay its success, that *The Wicker Man* was nevertheless much before its time.[2] I want to describe the genesis of the project; in so doing I have to rely on memory, and I have to some extent to speak on behalf of Tony because he is no longer with us.

Tony and I met in 1962, when he was sent to New York by J. Walter Thomson, then the world's largest and most influential

---

[1] University of Glasgow, Crichton Campus, Dumfries, July 14-15 2003.

[2] For further details of Deeley's alleged obstruction, see Brown, *Inside 'The Wicker Man'*, pp. 100-08, pp. 126-27, pp. 201-04; Bartholomew, 'The Wicker Man', pp. 38-42, p. 46.

advertising agency, to invite me to come to England and ultimately form a new television production company with him, which we called Hardy, Shaffer and Associates. Within five years our company, Hardy Shaffer, had branches in New York, Frankfurt, Paris, Milan, as well as London, and had become quite a big business.[3]

Over that same period of time, Tony's twin brother, Peter, wrote *Five Finger Exercises* (1959), *The Royal Hunt of the Sun* (1964), *Black Comedy* (1965), *White Lies* (1967), *The Battle of Shrivings* (1970), and was starting on *Equus* (1973). Although probably not as trendy as John Osborne, Arnold Wesker and co., he is arguably the most successful and eloquent English-speaking playwright of our time.[4] Tony, who had the same desire to write for the theatre, had written *The Savage Parade* (1963) and *For Years I Couldn't Wear My Black*, a spoof on the advertising industry.[5] Neither quite made it, although Tony's talent was very evident. Peter, seeing his twin's disappointment, and believing in his talent, proposed that Tony should retire from active work in our company and concentrate on writing. We all agreed on this course of action, but in return for my assuming the additional burden of running Hardy Shaffer without Tony, we agreed that we would make a feature film together. That film became *The Wicker Man*.

When Tony did write his next play, it was an instant hit. He first called it *Anyone for Tennis?*, but Michael White, the producer, didn't care for the title (quite rightly) and it became *Sleuth* (1970). The importance of *Sleuth* as an antecedent to *The Wicker Man* is hard to exaggerate.[6] *Sleuth* is the quintessential games-player's play. For those who are innocent of this dangerous obsession, games-playing,

---

[3] See Brown, *Inside 'The Wicker Man'*, p. 21.

[4] Critical studies of Peter Shaffer include MacMurraugh-Kavanagh, *Peter Shaffer*; Giankaris, *Peter Shaffer*.

[5] The alternative title of *For Years I Couldn't Wear My Black* is *Widow's Weeds*; it was not produced on stage until 1977.

[6] While Peter Shaffer's theatrical career has to date received more critical attention than that of his brother Anthony, some critical/biographical source material is available for the latter: see Klein, *Peter and Anthony Shaffer*; Anthony Shaffer, *So What Did You Expect?*

like gambling, is the diversion of those who would emulate the gods and intervene anonymously – however briefly – in the fate of another person. It is of course not to be confused with the playing of games on computers, manufactured for would-be amateur generals, politicians, tycoons, etc. The pawns in the games of which I speak must be human. John Fowles' *The Magus* (1966), Terry Southern's *The Magic Christian* (1959) and Alexandre Dumas' *The Count of Monte Cristo* (1845) all deal in such games, sometimes better known as 'revenges'. Throughout our long association, Tony and I indulged in a series of tit-for-tat games in which each sought to outdo the other.

One of the threads that informs *The Wicker Man* is 'the game', the hunter leading the hunted. But it is only one thread; there are others just as important. Tony and Peter Shaffer and I were great aficionados of the 'Gothic' horror films coming out of Hammer Films at the time.[7] They were a cult if ever there was one. We enjoyed examining the camp world of black magic and glamorous women cast largely because of their long white necks and heaving bosoms; we admired charismatic actors like Christopher Lee, with his marvellous voice and hypnotic eyes.

Discussing one of these films one day, Tony and I remarked how extraordinary it was that witchcraft and all the mythology surrounding it is just a peek, as it were, into the coffin of the old religion, where the faith of our long-ago forefathers is among the undead.[8] Centuries of Christian propaganda had driven it underground, perverted it in many cases, equated everything to do with it as evil, the work of the Devil. But the really astonishing thing, we concluded, is that so much of it survives out in the open and is part of our everyday life here and now. All our superstitions,

---

[7] Hardy here refers to the studio whose prolific feature output between *The Curse of Frankenstein* (1957) and *To the Devil a Daughter* (1976) became, and to a significant extent still remains, synonymous with the idea of a distinctively 'British', or perhaps more properly, 'English', horror cinema. For further details, see Hutchings, *Hammer and Beyond*; Meikle and Koetting, *A History of Horrors*; Chibnall and Petley, *British Horror Cinema*.

[8] See Bartholomew, 'The Wicker Man', pp. 10-13.

dozens of nursery rhymes, but most important of all, the old religion, survive incorporated into Christianity, and certainly in Judaism. Christmas and Easter are redolent of Celtic Paganism. It took Frazer huge research to trace the series of steps humankind has taken, linking its variegated modern beliefs to their remarkably universal beginnings. Francis Ford Coppola has the Marlon Brando figure in *Apocalypse Now* (1979), at the end of the film's long, long journey, skulking sleeplessly in the heart of darkness with – in case we miss the point – an open copy of *The Golden Bough* beside him.[9] He is the king of the sacred grove who cannot sleep because there will always be another coming to win his crown. It is all in Frazer.

But first we needed a plot. Tony and Peter had written and published detective stories when they were at Cambridge. Tony was adept at spinning the web of deceit to confound the police; *Sleuth*'s anti-hero believes he has thought of everything. But what if, Tony then proposed, the police themselves – himself – are the victims? The clues the policeman finds, then, are indeed pertinent; but what neither he nor the audience can believe is that *he* is the victim and the crime has not yet occurred. That is the inspiration at the core of *The Wicker Man*.

Tony and I spent a whole, and, I must confess, very bibulous weekend figuring out how the plot would work, who would do what and to whom. As inky schoolboys we had both been forced to cram Roman history and Latin. It is, after all, one of the juicier reports from Germanicus' dispatch to the Emperor on the barbarians

---

9   See Brown, *Inside 'The Wicker Man'*, pp. 24-27. Scottish anthropologist Sir James Frazer (1854-1941) is best known for his seminal work *The Golden Bough: A Study in Magic and Religion* (4 eds., 1890-1922), an incredibly ambitious comparative study of religion and mythology in a global context. The immediate relevance of Frazer's text(s) – *The Golden Bough* expanded from 2 volumes to 12 between 1890 and 1915 – to *The Wicker Man* relates to the author's central hypothesis. This was that all known mythologies and religions (including Christianity) essentially developed from a single originary myth, a cult of fertility involving the worship and periodic sacrifice of a sacred king-figure, surrogate for a solar deity, who 'died' at harvest time, only to be reincarnated every spring. For further details, see Ackerman and Frazer, *J.G. Frazer*. See also Hardy's comments in Bartholomew, 'The Wicker Man', pp. 10-11.

that they sacrifice their enemies to their gods, in wicker men.[10] We had promised ourselves to do a film together, a fitting curtain to our partnership in Hardy Shaffer, now to be wound up. Tony intended to write more for the theatre and I wanted to return to the USA, to mix writing fiction with journalism and television. Peter Snell, then, and now once more, CEO of British Lion Films, read the first draft of the screenplay of The Wicker Man and had the vision to see that the film could be an extraordinary breakthrough, a kind of antithesis of the Hammer Horror films which would be, if anything, more scary.[11]

While I was spending a spell in hospital recovering from illness and culling Frazer for more material, Peter got Christopher Lee to read the script. This resulted in our star, the perfect Lord Summerisle, being the film's most ardent advocate from the start.[12]

Although much effort had gone into recreating a Pagan faith for our times, we had spent less thought on Howie's Christian faith. We knew that the Church of Scotland had beliefs that, while profoundly Christian, did not work so well with the plot as would the faith of the Episcopalian Church. We needed to highlight the sacrifice part of the Communion service, the blessed blood and body of Jesus Christ that Howie consumes symbolically. Taking bread and wine from the priest could only take place in an Episcopalian church. Episcopalian churches do exist in Scotland, but they are rather rare, and yet we felt compelled to use one, for the potent imagery of Christ's sacrifice. Edward Woodward, who played Howie so superbly, was a devout Christian. He was instinctively able to help me as director in interpreting the kind of faith his policeman character would certainly have

---

[10] Germanicus Caesar (15 BC-AD 19) was a Roman general who campaigned extensively in northern Europe in the later years of his short life. Elsewhere, Hardy also notes the influence of 'eyewitness' reports in Julius Caesar's The Gallic Wars (c. 58-51 BC) that Druidic cultures used wicker men to immolate human sacrificial offerings. See Bartholomew, 'The Wicker Man', p. 10.

[11] Shaffer's marked contemporary hostility to the classification of The Wicker Man as a 'Hammer Horror film' can be gauged from his comments contained in Bartholomew, 'The Wicker Man', p. 14; see also his retrospective comments quoted in Brown, Inside 'The Wicker Man', pp. 39-41.

[12] See Bartholomew, 'The Wicker Man', pp. 32-34; Lee, 'A Letter from Lord Summerisle'.

possessed. There were things he just wouldn't do, wouldn't say: 'Somebody of that faith would not do this'. One accepted Woodward's intuitions – he was, after all, living the character.

How many people see the connection of this Communion with the Wicker Man scene at the end is questionable. But that brings me to the final thread that we believed would make this film unique in its way. We wanted people to join in the work of the detective. His journey through the film is sown with clues, if a viewer can only read them, but it is a film filled with puzzles for those who cannot. But yet we don't cheat: there are always answers for the audience, if they look for them. Why are the pregnant women touching the trees? Why did the old people in the deaths registry have names from the Bible when everybody else is called after flora or fauna? Why does the woman in the ruined church have a baby at her breast but an egg in her free hand? All this puzzlement would be, we believed, part of the entertainment. As it happens, it is often what takes people back to see the film a second time, or to read the book. It is another factor in making *The Wicker Man* a film with a cult; at least that is what I believe.

Amongst the most important elements, and one that tended to be ignored by many critics who lauded *The Wicker Man*, was the music. Few realise that in the film, quite apart from its mood music, there are thirteen musical numbers which are sung and danced by the cast with the town band on screen. I always regretted this lack of recognition, which has, thankfully, ended in recent years. The work of the late Paul Giovanni as composer[13] is among the finest contributions made to the film, and Peter Shaffer's deft de-bowdlerisations set just the right tone of sexy lyricism.[14]

The music was a joy to research; Cecil Sharp's folk music

[13] Giovanni's creative contribution to *The Wicker Man*, with accompanying commentary from the composer himself, is detailed extensively in Bartholomew, 'The Wicker Man', pp. 34-36. A restored stereo version of Giovanni's original score for the film was eventually released on compact disc by Silva Screen in September 2002: for further details, see Collis, 'Up in smoke'. For critical response to this release, see Anon, 'Review: *The Wicker Man*', in *Music From The Movies*; Anon, 'Review: *The Wicker Man*', in *Film Score Monthly*.

[14] See Gary Carpenter's introductory comments to his contribution in the present volume.

publications[15] list many of the songs used, although some of the origins are blurred by the mists of time. Sharp was one of those eager Victorians who went around collecting things and annotating and making endless lists. He collected songs all over the British Isles and also in North America, where of course the immigrants had taken them; over hundreds of years they had varied slightly, rather like plants growing in different parts of the world but from the same origin. The trouble was that all these songs tended to be a bit sexy and had Pagan origins. Unfortunately, Queen Victoria, who was rather keen on folk songs, heard some and said that she wanted a complete collection of Sharp's work, whereupon he went into a complete panic and bowdlerised the whole lot. They were then published in the official edition, which was presented to Her Majesty, who was apparently pleased to have them. But they remained in this new bowdlerised edition, so that Peter had to 'un-bowdlerise' them to make them work for the film, and I suspect he did further research on returning them to their original versions.

We are planning a new film in the same genre as *The Wicker Man*. It is called *Cowboys for Christ*, and will star Christopher Lee and Sean Astin, Sam in *The Lord of the Rings* trilogy (2001-03). It is not a sequel or a prequel to *The Wicker Man*, and shares none of the same characters. It can be said to be about American innocents abroad and what can befall them, and as such, it is fairly topical. There will shortly be a website for *Cowboys for Christ*, telling more.[16]

---

[15] Cecil Sharp (1854-1921) was arguably the most influential early 20th century collector and critic of English folk song material. Key published collections and criticism include *English Folk-Song: Some conclusions* (1907 and subsequent eds.) and *The Morris Book: A history of Morris dancing* (1907 and subsequent eds.). For further details, see Karpeles, *Cecil Sharp*; Harker, *Fakesong*.

[16] In July 2003, Hardy was assembling production finance for a new film, provisionally titled *May Day*, now to be called *Cowboys for Christ*; he discusses this project further in the interview with Jonathan Murray in this volume. The movie is currently classified on industry website The Internet Movie Database as due to go into production in March 2006, with Christopher Lee and Vanessa Redgrave taking lead roles. For further details, see The Internet Movie Database, 'May Day (2005)'; for perhaps the earliest film trade press account of this new project, see Bing, 'Inside Move'. The accompanying novelisation, *Cowboys for Christ* is published by Luath Press.

Some words of Benjamin Disraeli will serve equally well as an introduction to *Cowboys for Christ* as they did for the book of *The Wicker Man*: 'Man is born to believe, and if no Church comes forward with its title deeds of truth, sustained in the traditions of sacred ages and by the convictions of countless generations, to guide him, he will find altars and idols in his own heart and in his own imagination'.

Bibliography

Ackerman, R. and Frazer, R., *J. G. Frazer: His life and work and the making of 'The Golden Bough'* (London: Palgrave MacMillan, 2001).

Anon, 'Review: *The Wicker Man*', *Film Score Monthly*, 7.8, October 2002, pp. 45-46.

Anon, 'Review: *The Wicker Man*', *Music From The Movies*, 35.6, 2002, pp. 69-70.

Bartholomew, D., 'The Wicker Man', *Cinefantastique*, 6.3, Winter 1977, pp. 4-18, pp. 32-46.

Bing, J., 'Inside Move: *Wicker* pair scotches notion of pic as remake', 17 April 2002, http://www.variety.com/index.asp?layout=upsell_article&articleID=VR1117865603&cs=1 [Accessed 10 January 2005].

Brown, A., *Inside 'The Wicker Man': The morbid ingenuities* (London: Sidgwick and Jackson, 2000).

Caesar, J., *Gallic War: Conquest of Gaul* (London: Penguin, 1982).

Chibnall, S. and Petley, J., eds., *British Horror Cinema* (London: Routledge, 2001).

Collis, C., 'Up in smoke', *The Daily Telegraph* (arts section), 23 May 1998, p. 1.

Frazer, J., *The Golden Bough: A study in magic and religion* (Mineola, NY: Dover, 2002).

Giankaris, C. J., *Peter Shaffer* (Basingstoke: Macmillan, 1992).

Harker, D., *Fakesong: The manufacture of British 'folksong'* (Milton Keynes: Open University Press, 1985).

Hutchings, P., *Hammer and Beyond: The British horror film* (Manchester: MUP, 1993).

Internet Movie Database, The, 'Cowboys for Christ (2005)', http://www.imdb.com/title/tt0323808/

Karpeles, M., *Cecil Sharp. His life and work* (London: Routledge, 1967).

Klein, D. A., *Peter and Anthony Shaffer: A reference guide* (Boston: G. K. Hall, 1982).

Lee. C., 'A Letter From Lord Summerisle', *Cinefantastique,* 6-7.4-1, Spring 1978, p. 60.

MacMurraugh-Kavanagh. M. K., *Peter Shaffer: Theatre and drama* (Basingstoke, Macmillan, 1992).

Meikle, D. with Koetting, C. T., *A History of Horrors: The rise and fall of Hammer* (Lanham MD/London: Scarecrow, 1996).

Shaffer, A., *So What Did You Expect?: A memoir* (London: Picador, 2001).

Sharp, C., *English Folk-Song: Some conclusions,* 4th ed (London: Wakefield, 1972).

_____, *The Morris Book: A history of Morris dancing* (London: Wakefield, 1974-5).

The Wicker Man, May Day and the Reinvention of Beltane

Richard Sermon

Folklore and Paganism

ROBIN HARDY AND ANTHONY SHAFFER's film *The Wicker Man* (1973) appears to have been largely inspired by two main sources. The first, though disputed by the film makers, was the novel *Ritual* (1967) by David Pinner, for which Hardy and Shaffer acquired the rights before commencing work on the film.[1] Whilst many elements in the book are quite different to *The Wicker Man*, a number of its themes are strikingly similar. In the book a police detective investigates the ritual murder of a young girl in a remote Cornish village. The Pagan beliefs and strange practices of the local community lead the main character into an ever more dangerous world. There is also a sensual young woman who tries to seduce the policeman, and the image of a hare is used to represent the murdered girl. In the film the events are relocated to a fictional Scottish island, with pagan and folkloric motifs employed to a far greater extent. In developing these motifs, Hardy and Shaffer drew upon the work of anthropologist Sir James Frazer (1854-1941), who interpreted a wide range of folk customs as having ancient Pagan origins. Between 1890 and 1915 Frazer published his 12 volume text *The Golden Bough*, with the widely available abridgement coming out in 1922. A monumental study in comparative folklore, magic, and religion, it showed parallels between the rites and beliefs of early cultures and those of Christianity. Its basic proposition was that human

---

[1] Brown, *Inside 'The Wicker Man'*, p. 14.

thought and behaviour have evolved from the magical to the religious through to the scientific, and that the archetypal ritual is the sacrifice of the tribal priest-king.

Table 1: Various Motifs Employed in The Wicker Man

Sympathetic Magic

Pregnant women touching the blossom

Beetle tethered to a nail

Breast feeding while holding an egg

Hanging the naval string on a tree

Placing a frog in the mouth/throat

Carrying out the image of death

Hand of Glory (severed hand)

Coins over the eyes of a corpse

Celtic Mythology

Nuada (Gaelic sun god)

Shoney (Gaelic sea god)

Salmon of Knowledge
(Fenian Cycle)

Avellunau (Welsh Pomona?)

Classical References

Wicker Man (Caesar and Strabo)

Druid Priest with sickle and mistletoe (Pliny)

Customs and Folk Characters

Maypole (ribbons are a 19th century addition)

May Queen (Queen of the May)

Fool with an inflated bladder
(Sword and Morris dancing)

Sword Dancers (Yorkshire, Durham and Northumberland)

Men holding Antlers (Abbots Bromley Horn Dancers)

Hobby Horse (Minehead Horse with Oseberg Ship Head)

Teaser (Padstow Hobby Horse)

Jack in the Green (associated with chimney sweeps)

Green Man (well known inn sign)

John Barleycorn (ballad and inn sign)

Corn Dollies (found throughout Europe)

March Hares (hares' 'mad' mating season)

Jumping through Midsummer bonfires

Weird Women (Anglo-Saxon *Wyrd* or fatal sisters)

Modern Paganism	Songs
Re-use of prehistoric stone circles	'The Highland Widow's Lament' (Burns)
Jumping through the 'need' fire	
	'The Rigs o' Barley' (Burns)
Festivals	'The Landlord's Daughter' (folk song)
Beltane (Gaelic spring festival)	
May Day (first recorded in Lincoln in 1244)	'Gently Johnny' (folk song)
	'The Tinker of Rye' (folk song)
Lammas (Anglo-Saxon *Hlafmœsse* or Loaf-mass)	'Oranges and Lemons' (nursery rhyme)
Harvest Festival (19th century revival)	'Miri it is while Summer ilast' (13th century song)
	'Summer is Icumen in' (13th century song)

As a result, the film includes a rich mix of Frazer's sympathetic magic, gods from Celtic mythology, classical accounts of the Druids and modern Pagan practices, as well as folk customs, songs and festivals (see Table 1). Lord Summerisle explains the existence of such practices on the island to Sergeant Howie when he describes his 'free thinking mid-Victorian' grandfather, who re-introduced Paganism to the islanders, 'giving the people back their joyous old gods'. These practices include a number of mainly, but not exclusively, English folk traditions and customs. The most obvious of these appear in the procession towards the climax of the film (see Fig. 1) and include:

The Hobby Horse, of which surviving examples include the Padstow 'Obby Oss', the Minehead hobby horse and 'Hob Nob' in Salisbury. The Summerisle horse is more like the Minehead example, but interestingly appears to have a version of the Oseberg Viking ship head (dragon) bolted onto the front.

The Teaser is a character associated with the Padstow 'Obby Oss' and leads the horse in its May Day procession. But with the usual Summerisle twist the Teaser is transformed into a Druid priest(ess)

complete with golden sickle and mistletoe, as described by the Roman historian Pliny the Elder.[2]

The Fool with his inflated bladder is found in many of the English dance traditions, including Morris dancing, sword dancing and the Abbots Bromley Horn Dance. In the film this character is clearly identified as both the 'king for a day' and Mr Punch with his exaggerated hunchback.

Sword Dancers, whose traditional form of dance ends with the interlocking of swords to form a star or 'knot', are found mainly in the northern counties of Yorkshire, Durham and Northumberland. On Summerisle the scene is given a more Scottish flavour with the six dancers wearing kilts and carrying claymore swords.

The Men with Antlers are almost certainly based on the Abbots Bromley Horn Dance from Staffordshire, which is performed each year on Wakes Monday in September. Their present costumes are a 19th century addition but nevertheless include a fool whose costume is very similar to that used in the film.

Jack in the Green was a foliate figure often associated with chimney sweeps, with surviving examples known in Bristol and Hastings. In the film's May Day procession Jack is carried along in a horse drawn cart.

An early illustration of these dance traditions can be found on the Betley Window from Staffordshire, now in the Victoria and Albert Museum. It contains 12 diamond shaped painted panes depicting a late medieval Morris dance or *masque* (see Fig. 2). It is believed to date from the early 16th century and includes a hobby horse, fool, maypole and Morris dancers. The significance of such 'ritual' dances is explained in the film when Sergeant Howie consults a book on folklore in the Summerisle Library:

> May Day Festivals – Primitive man lived and died by his harvest. The purpose of his spring ceremonies was to ensure a plentiful autumn. Relics of these fertility dramas are to be found all over Europe. In Great Britain, for example, one can still see harmless

---

2 Pliny the Elder, *Natural History*, XVI, p. 95.

versions of them danced in obscure villages on May Day. Their cast includes many alarming characters: a man-animal or hobby horse who canters at the head of the procession charging at the girls, a man-woman, a sinister teaser, played by the community leader or priest, and a man-fool, 'Punch', the most complex of all the symbolic figures, the privileged simpleton and 'king for a day'. Six swordsmen follow these figures and at the climax of the ceremony lock their swords together in a clear symbol of the sun. In pagan times however, these dances were not simply picturesque jigs, they were frenzied rites ending in a sacrifice by which the dancers hoped desperately to win over the goddess of the fields. In good times they offered produce to the gods and slaughtered animals, but in bad years, when the harvest had been poor, the sacrifice was a human being. In some cultures it would be the king himself, in others their most beloved virgin, and very often he or she would be kept hidden for months preceding this ceremony; just as the sun is hidden from earth in winter. Methods of sacrifice differed. Sometimes the victim would be drowned in the sea, or burned to death in a huge sacrificial bonfire. Sometimes the six swordsmen ritually beheaded the virgin. The chief priest then skinned the child, and wearing the still warm skin like a mantle, led the rejoicing crowds through the streets. The priest thus represented the goddess reborn and guaranteed another successful harvest next year.[3]

This text, though fictional, could almost have been taken verbatim from Frazer's *The Golden Bough*. It parallels 'primitive' beliefs with modern folk customs, and includes the sacrifice of the tribal priest-king as the central ritual. Whilst still popular in New Age and Neo-Pagan circles, Frazer's work has now been largely rejected by most anthropologists. However, in the 1970s Morris dancing and sword dancing were still thought by many to be the remnants of pre-Christian death and fertility rituals. More recent work suggests that the majority of our folk customs are unlikely to have ancient Pagan origins, with many first appearing in the late medieval period. This would include the work of Ronald Hutton, who has made a

---

[3]   Transcribed from *The Wicker Man* ([1973] 2002).

special study of ancient religion and the ritual year in the British Isles.[4] Nevertheless Frazer's ideas have exerted huge influence on modern literature and culture, as *The Wicker Man* demonstrates.

May Day and Beltane

The events in the film take place just before and during May Day, which is equated with the Pagan festival of Beltane, one of Frazer's 'fire festivals' in the 'Celtic Calendar'. When Sergeant Howie is examining girls' names in the school register the page is headed 'Belthane Term', whilst outside the boys dance around a maypole. The Celts are first recorded in the 5th century BC by the Greek historian Herodotus, who locates them in the area of the upper Danube.[5] Later Roman historians referred to a number of peoples within their empire as being either Celts or Gauls. In the 19th century archaeologists attempted to find evidence of these early Celts in central Europe, and identified two possible cultures named after the locations in which they were first discovered, Hallstatt and La Tène.[6] However, the Celtic language group was only defined by that name at the beginning of the 18th century by Edward Lhuyd, then curator of the Ashmolean Museum in Oxford,[7] and its relationship to these archaeological cultures is still a subject of much debate.[8] Nevertheless, at their greatest extent, what we now call Celtic languages were spoken throughout northern Italy, France, Spain, Britain and Ireland.

The following passage comes from the 10th to 11th century collection of Irish heroic tales known as the Ulster Cycle. During his wooing of Emer (*Tochmarc Emire*), the hero Cúchulainn is required to sleep for a year before she will agree to marry him. In describing

---

4   Hutton, *Pagan Religions of the Ancient British Isles*; *The Rise and Fall of Merry England*; *The Stations of the Sun*.
5   Herodotus, *The Histories*, p. 142.
6   Renfrew, *Archaeology and Language*, pp. 211-49.
7   Lhuyd, *Archæologia Britannica*, I.
8   James, *The Atlantic Celts*.

the year Emer also provides the earliest recorded reference to all four of the Irish pagan festivals that marked the changing of the seasons:

> 'No man will travel this country,' she said, 'who hasn't gone sleepless from Samain, when the summer goes to its rest, until Imbolc, when the ewes are milked at spring's beginning; from Imbolc to Beltane at the summer's beginning and from Beltane to Brón Trogain, earth's sorrowing autumn.'[9]

Three of these festival names have survived in Irish, Manx and Scots Gaelic, as the month names for May, August and November. However, in later sources Brón Trogain is known by the name Lúgnasad (see Table 2). In 1897 an important discovery was made at Coligny, near Lyons in France, when numerous fragments of a bronze Gaulish calendar were found, dating to the 2nd century AD. The calendar consisted of 12 lunar months (and two intercalary or leap months); however, the month names were very different to those recorded in the other Celtic languages, apart from Samonios which appears to be cognate with the Old Irish festival Samain (see Table 3).

Table 2: Old Irish Festivals

Old Irish	Manx Gaelic	Scots Gaelic	Irish	Interpretation
Imbolc	–	–	–	Ewes milking
Beltane	Boaldyn	Bealltainn	Bealtaine	Bright fire
Lúgnasad	Luanistyn	Lùnasdal	Lúnasa	Lug's festival
Samain	Sauin	Samhainn	Samhna	Summer end

Table 3: Coligny Calendar Months

Coligny	Reconstruction	Equivalent	Interpretation
SAMON	Samonios	Oct/Nov	Summer end/Seed time
DVMAN	Dumannios	Nov/Dec	Dark time
RIVROS	Riuros	Dec/Jan	Frost time

---

9 Kinsella, *The Tain*, p. 27.

Coligny	Reconstruction	Equivalent	Interpretation
ANAGAN	Anagantios	Jan/Feb	Home time
OGRON	Ogronios	Feb/Mar	Cold time
CVTIOS	Cutios	Mar/Apr	Wind time
GIAMON	Giamonios	Apr/May	Winter end/Shoots time
SIMIVIS	Simivisonnos	May/Jun	Light time
EQVOS	Equos	Jun/Jul	Horse time
ELEMBIV	Elembiuios	Jul/Aug	Harvest time
AEDRINI	Aedrinios	Aug/Sep	Hot time
CANTLOS	Cantlos	Sep/Oct	Song time

Table 4: Celtic Revival Calendar

Celtic Year	Date	Assumed Equivalent
Winter Solstice	21 December	Yule
Imbolc	1 February	Lent
Spring Equinox	21 March	Easter
Beltane	1 May	May Day
Summer Solstice	21 June	Midsummer
Lúgnasad	1 August	Lammas
Autumn Equinox	22 September	Harvest
Samain	1 November	Halloween

In the 19th century, during the 'Celtic Revival', these early Irish festivals were rediscovered by folklorists and academics, such as Sir James Frazer, who attempted to reconstruct a pan-Celtic year that was said to have existed not only in Ireland and Scotland, but also throughout Britain and the former Celtic speaking parts of Europe. This 'Celtic Calendar' was believed to have included the winter and summer solstices, and the spring and autumn equinoxes, as well as the four recorded festivals that marked the changing seasons. In addition, it was thought that bonfires had been a central part of all these festivals, giving rise to the idea of the fire festivals.[10] The

---

[10]   Frazer, *The Golden Bough*, pp. 609-41.

resulting calendar (see Fig. 3 and Table 4) has been used extensively since the 19th century to explain the origins of various English folk customs and festivals including May Day.[11]

However, there are a number of significant problems with this reconstructed calendar. Firstly, while Imbolc, Beltane, Lúgnasad and Samain are found in the Goidelic branch of the Celtic language group (Irish, Manx and Scots Gaelic) they are not found in the Brithonic branch (Welsh, Cornish and Breton), which therefore casts doubt on the claim that these were pan-Celtic festivals.[12] Secondly, the early Irish texts do not mention festivals on the solstices or equinoxes, hence the lack of Old Irish names for these. Thirdly, these festivals, which were not necessarily observed by the Celtic Britons, are assumed to have passed from them into English folk tradition. So it would appear that the 'Celtic Calendar' is in reality a recent academic construction. Still, the concept is now so deeply embedded in both popular and academic belief, that it is repeated throughout the literature on Celtic culture, history and archaeology, but with no reference to original source material.[13]

If, on the other hand, we examine the Germanic language group, which includes English (and Lowland Scots), we find a far greater level of agreement (see Table 5). Such broad agreement among the Germanic languages, when compared with the Celtic languages, would suggest that a common year is more likely to have existed in the Germanic rather than Celtic speaking parts of Europe.[14] Furthermore, May traditions in England appear to have been very different to Beltane traditions recorded in Scotland and Ireland. May games were first recorded in 1244 when the Bishop of Lincoln, Robert Grosseteste, complained of '*ludos quos vocant Inductionem Maii*' or 'games which they call the Bringing in of May'.[15] May Day was celebrated on various dates in May and traditionally marked the

---

[11]   MacNeill, *The Festival of Lughnasa.*

[12]   Hutton, *Pagan Religions of the Ancient British Isles*, pp. 408-11.

[13]   Cunliffe, *The Ancient Celt*, pp. 188-90.

[14]   Sermon, 'The Celtic Calendar and the Anglo-Saxon Year'.

[15]   Luard, *Roberti Grosseteste Epistolae*, CVII, 317.

Table 5: Common Germanic Season and Festival Names

Old English	Old Frisian	Middle Dutch	Old High German	Old Norse
Geola	–	–	–	Jól
Lencten	–	Lentin	Lengizin	Vár
Eastron	Asteron	–	Ostarun	–
Sumor	Sumur	Somer	Sumar	Sumar
Middansumor	Middesumur	Midsomer	Mittesumar	Miórsumar
Hærfest	Herfst	Herfst	Herbist	Haust
Winter	Winter	Winter	Wintar	Vetr
Middanwinter	Middewinter	Midwinter	Mittewintar	Miórvetr

English	Low Saxon	Dutch	German	Swedish
Yule	–	Joelfeest	Julfest	Jul
Lent	–	Lente	Lenz	Vår
Easter	Oostern	–	Ostern	–
Summer	Sommer	Zomer	Sommer	Sommar
Midsummer	Midsommer	Midzomer	Mittsommer	Midsommar
Harvest	Harvst	Herfst	Herbst	Höst
Winter	Winter	Winter	Winter	Vinter
Midwinter	Midwinter	Midwinter	Mittwinter	Midvinter

beginning of summer. May customs included the May Queen and garland, maypole dancing, May Day carols and washing your face in the May morning dew, as well as Morris dancing, hobby horses and Jack in the Green. Beltane traditions in Ireland (*Bealtaine*) and Highland Scotland (*Bealltainn*) were very different and involved the lighting of bonfires and rites to purify livestock such as cattle and sheep.[16] A somewhat lurid, if not hostile, description of the English May traditions and Morris dancing is provided by the puritan Phillip Stubbes in his *Anatomy of Abuses*:

---

[16] Ross, *The Folklore of the Scottish Highlands*, pp. 134-38.

35

All the young men and maids, old men and wives, run gadding over night to the woods, groves, hills, and mountains, where they spend all the night in pleasant pastimes; and in the morning they return, bringing with them birch and branches of trees, to deck their assemblies withal. For there is a great Lord present amongst them, as superintendent and Lord over their pastimes and sports, namely Satan, prince of hell. But the chiefest jewel they bring from thence is their May-pole, which they bring home with great veneration, as thus. They have twenty or forty yoke of oxen, every ox having a sweet nose-gay of flowers placed on the tip of his horns, and these oxen draw home this May-pole (this stinking idol, rather), which is covered all over with flowers and herbs, bound round about with strings, from the top to the bottom, and sometimes painted with variable colours, with two or three hundred men, women and children following it with great devotion. And thus being reared up, with handkerchiefs and flags hovering on the top, they straw the ground round about, bind green boughs about it, set up summer halls, bowers, and arbours hard by it. And then fall they to dance about it, like as the heathen people did at the dedication of the Idols, whereof this is a perfect pattern, or rather the thing itself. I have heard it credibly reported by men of great gravity and reputation, that of forty, threescore, or a hundred maids going to the wood over night, there have scarcely the third part of them returned home again undefiled [. . .]

They [Morris dancers] bedeck themselves with scarves ribbons and laces hanged all over with gold rings, precious stones and other jewels; this done they tie about either leg twenty or forty bells, with rich handkerchiefs in their hands, and sometimes laid across their shoulders and necks, borrowed for the most part of their pretty Mopsies and loving Bessies for kissing them in the dark. Thus all things set in order, then they have hobby-horses, dragons and other antics, together with their gaudy pipers and thundering drummers to strike up the devils dance withal. Then march these heathen company towards the church and churchyard, their pipers piping, their drummers thundering, their stumps dancing, their bells jingling, their handkerchiefs swinging about their heads like madmen, their hobby-horses and other monsters skirmishing among the throng.[17]

---

[17] Stubbes, 1583, quoted in Frazer, *The Golden Bough*, p. 162.

The Wicker Man

The final scene of the film, with the islanders offering Sergeant Howie as a sacrifice to their gods Nuada and Avellunau, is based primarily on two classical sources from around the 1st century BC. The first is a passage in Julius Caesar's *Gallic Wars*, a personal account of his campaigns in ancient Gaul, which describes the Druids burning people alive in large human effigies as sacrificial offerings:

> The nation of all the Gauls is extremely devoted to superstitious rites; and on that account they who are troubled with unusually severe diseases, and they who are engaged in battles and dangers, either sacrifice men as victims, or vow that they will sacrifice them, and employ the Druids as the performers of those sacrifices; because they think that unless the life of a man be offered for the life of a man, the mind of the immortal gods can not be rendered propitious, and they have sacrifices of that kind ordained for national purposes. Others have figures of vast size, the limbs of which formed of osiers they fill with living men, which being set on fire, the men perish enveloped in the flames. They consider that the oblation of such as have been taken in theft, or in robbery, or any other offence, is more acceptable to the immortal gods; but when a supply of that class is wanting, they have recourse to the oblation of even the innocent.[18]

The second reference is by the Greek geographer and historian Strabo in his *Geography*, which incorporated both his own observations and earlier sources. Strabo refers not only to humans being burnt in these effigies but various animals as well:

> The Romans put a stop both to these customs and to the ones connected with sacrifice and divination, as they were in conflict with our own ways: for example, they [the Gallic peoples] would strike a man who had been consecrated for sacrifice in the back with a sword, and make prophecies based on his death-spasms; and they would not sacrifice without the presence of the Druids. Other kinds of human sacrifices have been reported as well: some

---

[18] Caesar, *De Bello Gallico*, 6,16.

men they would shoot dead with arrows and impale in the temples; or they would construct a huge figure of straw and wood, and having thrown cattle and all manner of wild animals and humans into it, they would make a burnt offering of the whole thing.[19]

The first illustration of these effigies was by Aylett Sammes (c.1636 to c.1679), an antiquary and historian who attempted to demonstrate the antiquity of British culture by linking Britain to the ancient Phoenicians. In his *Britannia Antiqua Illustrata* he described the 'Wicker Image', in which he stated that the ancient Britons (not just the Gauls) would burn their human sacrifices.[20] With the appearance of this illustration we have the basic design for all the subsequent examples of the wicker man. From the 18th century onwards this design was repeated many times in editions of Caesar's *Gallic Wars* and related works.

In *The Golden Bough* Frazer looks for surviving evidence of the wicker man in modern European folk traditions and identifies two possible candidates.[21] The first are dancing giants, a tradition found in many parts of the world. In Europe they are found especially in Catalonia, Flanders and Navarre, where they are a prominent feature of traditional, civic and religious celebrations. In Britain most were destroyed during the reformation or by the Puritans in the 17th century, but Salisbury's traditional giant St Christopher can still be seen in the city's museum (see Fig. 4). The second are animal burnings during various religious feasts in the Church calendar, in which cats appear to fare particularly badly (see Table 6). Frazer suggests that these two customs had a common origin, and that they are remnants of the wicker man sacrifices described by Caesar. He also points out that they are found in and around what was the province of Gaul. However, he offers no evidence that actually links these two practices.

When Hardy and Shaffer came to film their wicker man on

---

[19]   Strabo, *Geography* 4.1.13, quoted in Koch and Carey, *The Celtic Heroic Age*, p. 18.

[20]   Sammes, *Britannia Antiqua Illustrata,* pp. 104-05.

[21]   Frazer, *The Golden Bough*, pp. 652-58.

Table 6: Frazer's Giants and Animal Burnings

Giants	Animal Burnings
Antwerp	Alsace (cats)
Brabant	Ardenes (cats)
Brie	Gap (cats)
Burford	Luchon (snakes)
Chester	Meissen (horse head)
Coventry	Metz (cats)
Douay	Paris (cats)
Dunkirk	Russia (white cock)
Flanders	Thuringia (horse head)
London	Vosges (cats)
Paris	
Salisbury	

Burrowhead, they built a scaled down version for one man and assorted animals. However, the basic design is still that described by Aylett Sammes, which derives ultimately from Caesar and Strabo's classical descriptions. While there is a general consensus that human sacrifice was practised in Iron Age Europe,[22] Caesar's account of the wicker man refers only to practices in Gaul, and may have been simply Roman propaganda. Given that Strabo may have copied Caesar's earlier description, and the lack of any other supporting evidence, it begs the question whether anyone had actually built or burnt a wicker man before the autumn of 1972.

The Film's Legacy

While the film was itself influenced by contemporary thinking on Paganism and folklore in the 1970s, the film's imagery has since become the inspiration for many new celebrations. These include

---

[22]   Green, *Human Sacrifice in Iron Age Europe.*

the Burning Man Festival in Nevada (since 1986), the Beltane fire festival in Edinburgh (since 1988), and the Wickerman Festival in Kirkcudbrightshire (since 2002), along with a host of Neo-Pagan rites that can be found on the Internet. Further influences of the film can be seen in the rock band Iron Maiden's 'Wicker Man' single (released 2000), and the 'Pagan' army in the *Warrior Kings* computer game, which includes a Wicker Man, Maypole and Henge.

Interestingly, the film also appears to have inspired modern re-enactments at a number of reconstructed Iron Age settlements, where public events have included the burning of a wicker man. At the Peat Moor Centre near Glastonbury in Somerset, a wicker man is constructed every Samain (end of October) and burnt at dusk, while at Gillingham in Kent the Iron Age re-enactment group the 'Cantiaci' do the same at Beltane (beginning of May). At Castell Henllys in Pembrokeshire an Iron Age hill fort has been excavated and almost completely reconstructed. The site is run by the Pembrokeshire National Park and was used by the BBC for their living history programme 'Surviving the Iron Age' in 2000. This was a reality programme with a difference, where members of the public volunteered to live (if possible) as Iron Age people. To celebrate the end of their stay the volunteers constructed a wicker man, which they burnt at Samain. Since then Castell Henllyss has hosted a number wicker man burnings on Imbolc (beginning of February), Beltane, and Samain. Perhaps the best example, however, is at Butser Ancient Farm in Hampshire. Butser was founded by Dr Peter Reynolds in 1972, as an open-air laboratory for research into Prehistoric and Roman agriculture and building techniques, and was one of the first experimental archaeology centres. Over the last 25 years the burning of a wicker man on Beltane has become an annual fund raising event, complete with Druids and Morris men.

Having learnt about the event from their Internet pages I decided to visit the Butser Festival of Beltane 2003 with my family (see Fig. 5), and observed things for myself.[23] The event started at 6.30 in the evening, when we joined approximately 600 other visitors. A Druid

---

[23]   Butser Festival of Beltane (2003), www.butser.org.uk

priest and priestess officiated during proceedings, which began with the Victory Morris Men from Portsmouth dancing close to a Maypole in the centre of the farm. This was followed by a procession around the fields, where offerings were made to the gods to ensure a fruitful harvest. The procession also passed a wooden 'totem' in the form of a hare, while one of the participants was dressed as a Green Man. Before the main event visitors were entertained by fire-jugglers to the sound of African drums, along with a bar and barbecue and 'woad' face painting. As dusk fell the Druids put their burning torches to the 25ft high wicker man, which was quickly enveloped in flames and provided a spectacular climax to the evening. A subsequent press release explained that the wicker man was 'burnt as a sacrifice to ensure good fertility among crops and animals for this growing season'. The event was a great deal of fun and the family certainly enjoyed it. But consciously or otherwise, the staff at Butser appeared to be reproducing many of the elements found in the film – the association of modern folk tradition with ancient Paganism, May Day with Beltane, and of course the wicker man itself. At a site like Butser it has to be asked where public entertainment/theatre ends and where education begins. Is archaeology objectively shaping our understanding of the past, or is archaeology, like any other discipline, unavoidably influenced by popular culture?

Conclusions

If we deconstruct the various elements in both the film and these more recent festivals, we find that many of the underlying assumptions upon which they are based are now highly questionable. In the 1970s traditions like Morris dancing and sword dancing were still thought by many to be the remnants of pre-Christian death and fertility rituals. However, more recent research suggests that the majority of our folk customs are unlikely to have ancient Pagan origins. Since the 19th century the so-called 'Celtic Calendar' has often been used to explain various English folk customs and festivals including May Day, which was often equated with the festival Beltane. In reality, however, the 'Celtic Calendar' is a modern academic

construction. Furthermore, May traditions in England were very different to Beltane traditions recorded in Ireland and Highland Scotland. *The Wicker Man*'s most potent and lasting image has been that of the burning effigy that gives the film its title. Since the film's release in 1973 there has been a steady proliferation of wicker man burnings in Britain and America. However, Julius Caesar's account of this refers only to practices in Gaul, and may have been simply Roman propaganda. In the absence of any other evidence (from antiquity or more recent times), the very first wicker man may have been the one built and burnt on Burrowhead in the autumn of 1972. Nevertheless, the film's eclectic mix of imagery has had a profound effect on both popular and academic representations of our Pagan past.

Bibliography

Brown, A., *Inside 'The Wicker Man': The morbid ingenuities* (London: Sidgwick and Jackson, 2000).

Butser Festival of Beltane, www.butser.org.uk [Accessed April 2003].

Caesar, J. *De Bello Gallico*, trans. W. McDevitte and W. Bohn (New York: Harper and Brothers, 1869).

Cunliffe, B., *The Ancient Celts* (Oxford: Oxford University Press, 1997).

Frazer, J. G., *The Golden Bough* (Ware: Wordsworth Reference, 1922).

Green, M., 'Human Sacrifice in Iron Age Europe', *British Archaeology*, 38, (1998), www.britarch.ac.uk/ba/ba38/ba38feat.html [Accessed April 2003].

Hardy, R. (Director), *The Wicker Man – Special Edition Director's Cut* (Canal+, [1973] 2002).

Herodotus, *The Histories*, trans. A. Selincourt (London: Penguin, 1954).

Hutton, R., *Pagan Religions of the Ancient British Isles* (Oxford: Oxford University Press, 1991).

_____, *The Rise and Fall of Merry England* (Oxford: Oxford University Press, 1994).

_____, *The Stations of the Sun* (Oxford: Oxford University Press, 1996).

James, S., *The Atlantic Celts* (London: British Museum Press, 1999).

Kinsella, T., trans., *The Tain* (Oxford: Oxford University Press, 1970).

Koch, J. and Carey, J., eds., *The Celtic Heroic Age* (Malden, Massachusetts: Celtic Studies Publications, 1995).

Lhuyd, E., *Archæologia Britannica*, I (Oxford, 1707).

Luard H. R., ed., *Roberti Grosseteste Epistolae*, CVII (London: Longman, 1861), p. 317.

MacNeill, M., *The Festival of Lughnasa* (Oxford: Oxford University Press, 1962).

Pinner, D., *Ritual: Murder, witchcraft and paganism in a Cornish village* (London: Macmillan, 1967).

Pliny the Elder, *Natural History, XII-XVI*, trans. H. Rackham (Harvard: Loeb, 1958).

Renfrew, C., *Archaeology and Language* (London: Penguin, 1987).

Ross, A., *The Folklore of the Scottish Highlands* (London: Batsford, 1976).

Sammes, A., *Britannia Antiqua Illustrata*, (London: Thomas Roycroft, 1676).

Sermon, R., 'The Celtic Calendar and the Anglo-Saxon Year', *3rd Stone*, 43 (2002), pp. 32-39.

Ritualistic Behaviour in *The Wicker Man:* A classical and carnivalesque perspective on 'the true nature of sacrifice'

Paula James

THIS CONTRIBUTION FOLLOWS the terrifying trajectory of *The Wicker Man*'s hero, Neil Howie, from selection to sacrifice, with reference primarily to Greco-Roman rituals. Since participating in the stimulating *Wicker Man* conference I have looked at several features of the film afresh.[1] My perspective remains primarily a classical one, where I feel on safer ground. However, the origins of social ritual are not subjects that lend themselves to neat cultural packaging. The Greco-Roman timbre of the film was not consciously created (the emphasis is naturally on allegedly Celtic rituals) but elements of classical sacrifice can be detected as the plot unfolds. Howie's austerity at a time of joyful celebration poses him counter to the pursuit of pleasure in the community, suggesting his special role as outsider and as guiltless victim. This is both classical and carnivalesque in its conception.

When I first saw the film in its truncated version on television in the 1980s, I was struck by the interesting parallels it presented to an episode in an ancient (Latin) novel, namely *The Golden Ass* or *Metamorphoses* of Apuleius. The common denominator was selection for sacrifice and the victims' subsequent 'sacrificial' behaviour. For this reason (and in spite of the absence in the theatrical version of the more obvious early clues supplied in the restored director's

---

[1] '*The Wicker Man:* Rituals, Readings and Reactions' conference, University of Glasgow, Crichton Campus, 14-15 July 2003.

cut) I was quickly convinced that the luckless policeman was the one being prepared for some sort of ritual slaughter.[2] It was clear that like the protagonist of the ancient novel, Lucius, Neil Howie had been sought out and was being ritually prepared to play his central role in and for the community festival.[3]

For most commentators, the only Roman connection is Julius Caesar, who provided the ancient testimony on Celtic customs of sacrifice; he actually describes in his *Gallic Wars* a wicker construction for burning victims.[4] For those engaged in Celtic studies the existence of such wicker men as sacrificial structures is questionable. Indeed, the conflation of May Day rites one also finds in Frazer's *The Golden Bough* has been subjected to critical scrutiny,

---

[2]   In the restored version there are amused comments by police colleagues on Howie's virgin state and his devotion to his religion – to my mind this preliminary episode set on the mainland does not strengthen the film in terms of characterisation. They also set up too obvious an adult virgin sacrifice motif. The scene in the church is, however, significant as its refrain is taken up at the end of the film.

[3]   Robin Hardy and Anthony Shaffer drew their inspiration for the cultic practices of Summerisle from James Frazer's *The Golden Bough*, which conflates a variety of May Day and Beltane customs; see Brown in his foreword to the Hardy and Shaffer novel, *The Wicker Man*, p. xi. Robin Hardy emphasised the importance of *The Golden Bough* as a source in his address to *The Wicker Man* conference.

[4]   Caesar's report in *De Bello Gallico* 6,16 (cf. statements by Strabo and Diodorus Siculus) may have drawn from Posidonius' Celtic ethnography, so the vivid picture in *The Gallic Wars* is possibly Caesar adding colour to his account of Celtic practices. In the light of suspect testimony, Sermon (this volume) has suggested that the first wicker man to be constructed was the edifice created for the film. However, Caesar could have seen such a cage and witnessed its use for the slaughter of criminals and prisoners of war. Caesar did not need to justify conquest to the recipients of his work at Rome by demonising the Celts as practitioners of human sacrifice, but this display of knowledge about 'barbaric' rites would possibly have helped in the popularisation of these yearly reports from Gaul. See Wiseman, 'The Publication of *De Bello Gallico*', for the suggestion that Caesar's books on the war in Gaul may have been intended as dispatches from the front to be read to the general public and to keep the commander's profile public in his absence from Rome.

especially during the thirty years since *The Wicker Man*'s release. I leave the critique of Frazer to the experts. The point is that the islanders are bringing to life Frazer's anthropological text, *The Golden Bough*, rather than drawing on 'race memory' to resurrect ancient ritualistic practices. It is significant that they subsequently match and mimic in their masking costumes those figures Howie reads about and sees in the illustrations in the book on 'Celtic' May Day rituals at the local library.[5]

If I had written an extended version of the story to follow the film I would have suggested that there were Roman refinements added to this strange, chronologically displaced and hybrid carnival of death and renewal. These refinements would undoubtedly have been inspired by the ruler of the island. In countering Howie's censure about being a Pagan, Lord Summerisle admits to being 'a heathen, maybe, but not, I hope, an unenlightened one'. Summerisle could have incorporated Greco-Roman ingredients from his classical reading into the community's discourse of sacrifice. Lord Summerisle proudly informs Howie that the joyous old gods of Paganism were re-introduced into the community as a social expedient by his Victorian grandfather. There were plenty of joyous old gods to choose from in the ancient world. Whatever their provenance, the Greco-Roman features in the islanders' religious observations enrich and complicate the Celtic cocktail the community has concocted.

Howie has been singled out as a particularly appropriate candidate to 'purify' Summerisle and restore it to the gods' good graces by virtue of the social institutions he represents, as well as for his personal qualities. He is an outsider with authority and status and, as such, needs to be temporarily integrated into the community before he can function effectively and ritually in the final festival. He must also be manipulated into a show of willingness at crucial

---

5   The final scenes of the film give life and movement to the disturbing pictures. *The Wicker Man* is fascinating because it implies a reflection on this very process when the camera shares the 'story board' stills with the movie audience while keeping these sketches of scenes to come as a logical development of the internal narrative.

stages of the celebrations. In Greek and Roman rituals sacrificial animals were supposed to behave biddably and even to look joyful during the processions and the preparations for their slaughter. Human scapegoats were more likely to suffer exile than death but they too would disturb and damage the proceedings if they did not participate properly. In this respect Howie has to be induced to abide by the rules of a game he does not know he is playing.[6]

Human scapegoats (and Howie is very much in this mode) were normally part of the community, but there is evidence that strangers could briefly be integrated into the ranks of a society in order to play this role and to absorb and carry away the collective misfortune.[7] This was one way around the difficulty of sacrificing a valued member of the society: someone of little significance could be either artificially or temporarily promoted, or a recent guest could be made the important figurehead, in order to fulfil one's bargain with a god. The twentieth century policeman finds himself the victim in a religiously 'regressive' rite designed to appease the gods and restore success to the Summerisle crops. He functions as a scapegoat and is expelled from the community boundaries by death, rather than exile. He faces the true horror of a human forced to play the part usually taken by an animal that has been carefully chosen and nurtured for slaughter. The cinematically powerful 'merry dance' the community devises for the duped sergeant

---

[6] In his introductory contribution to the present volume Robin Hardy characterises the film more as detective thriller genre than as horror movie. The game the Summerisle inhabitants play with Howie, and the building of suspense in his search for the truth and for Rowan, evoke the twists and turns of Anthony Shaffer's highly successful play, *Sleuth*.

[7] I hesitate to use the word 'guilt' because of its Christian connotations. A more apt term is 'pollution'. The Summerisle people mimic ancient communities in their appeasement of gods they may have inadvertently offended. The need to purify their village to avert divine displeasure propels them into an elaborate charade; their chosen victim is unwittingly absorbing their ill fortune as he interacts with them. For variations in sacrificial scapegoat strategies see Bremmer, 'Scapegoat Rituals in Ancient Greece', *passim*.

is even more poignant if its distorted symbolic significance is recognised.[8]

It is spelt out in the novel *The Wicker Man,* which was written after the film, that Lord Summerisle has investigated Howie to ascertain that he is morally and ethically upright. Summerisle identifies Neil Howie as the right kind of adult to be offered up to the island's Celtic gods, but the islanders also need to be confident in his suitability. The whole community therefore has the opportunity to look him over once he arrives. Willow, the landlord's comely daughter, who is clearly a connoisseur in such matters, refers to him as her 'pretty sergeant'. By the end of the film we are told explicitly that Howie had been chosen as the sacrifice because, as a policeman, he embodies the authority of a king and that of the law. He has kept himself physically virginal and resisted Willow's attempt at seduction. In both the novel and the original screenplay, Lord Summerisle makes it explicit that this episode is a test which Howie has passed with flying colours: 'We offered you Willow, a 'dish' indeed to set before any king, but you, in defence of your virginity, rejected her, as we hoped you would. For it makes you doubly acceptable to the gods.'[9] In Greek and Roman sacrifice, willow is a highly charged wood symbolising a time of renewal. Willow is also the traditional wood for osiery and the supple seductress at the inn does seem almost to be coalescing with her name in her weaving dance around the room, when she tempts Howie on the second night of his stay. Ironically, willow re-appears in her other form to embrace Howie as part, we can assume, of his death-delivering wicker cage at the end of the film. In ancient scapegoat observances willow played its part as an infertility symbol and for apotropaic purposes; the rods of *agnus castus* were used to chase away famine. Criminals

---

[8]   My interpretation owes a great deal to McCreight ('Sacrificial Ritual in Apuleius' *Metamorphoses*'), who teased out symbolic sacrificial features in *The Golden Ass,* where Lucius is manipulated into playing the starring and humiliating part in the festival of Laughter. Lucius, like Howie, is looked over and approved: he is a handsome and well-groomed young stranger, the right kind of adult to perform the town's ritual.

[9]   Hardy and Shaffer, *The Wicker Man,* p. 269.

were whipped with the twigs of unproductive trees and the willow was one of these. It was known as *arbor infelix* – 'unlucky' or even 'baneful tree' – and also referred to the gallows in Roman times.[10] For early Christian writers the tree became a symbol of chastity; in the film's artificially created Pagan community, Willow, the woman, represents sexuality for its own sake.

Rowan, the missing girl, could be viewed as a representation of the newly fertile branch, hidden away but awaiting her entrance for 'tomorrow's tomorrow' (as Howie refers to May Day), while Willow is the fully blossomed and ostentatious symbol of the Spring Festival. Like Willow, Rowan offers her hand to the policeman, who poignantly trusts her to lead the way out of danger. Rowan's sister Myrtle is another teasing female.[11] When she hands the policeman her paintbrush 'to fill in the ears' of the hare, she is enticing him into the fantasy of her sister Rowan's metamorphosis. All these are superficially playful moments before the festival takes a serious turn.

With her matter of fact lesson on the veneration of the penis as phallic symbol, Miss Rose, the schoolteacher, mimics the persona of the policeman. On first appearance her demeanour and dress are modest and old-fashioned. She ought to be the policeman's natural ally but she is, as Howie quickly perceives, the rationaliser of the community's lascivious and godless behaviour. She reflects the authority of Lord Summerisle, as do all the 'pillars' of the community whom Howie encounters, from the doctor to the librarian to the public records officer. His interaction with these figures has a further significance as everyone he touches transfers another part

---

[10] Bremmer, 'Scapegoat Rituals in Ancient Greece', pp. 310-12. I am indebted to Jo Pearson, School of Religious and Theological Studies, Cardiff University, for her comments on my paper and especially her observations on season-ally symbolic wood.

[11] The myrtle branch and blossom were sacred to Greek Aphrodite (Roman Venus). Willow is called Aphrodite, goddess of Love, by Lord Summerisle in the Ash Buchanan sexual initiation scene, omitted from the theatrical version of the film. It is surely symbolically significant that *May* is the name of the Morrison sisters' mother.

of the community's misfortune to him in the time-honoured scape-goat tradition. A possible interpretation of his temporary integration into the village is that Howie will ultimately embody the pollution that has infected the community and their crops and carry this away with him when he dies. The fact that Howie has to be fooled into this role makes his situation all the more poignant.

With hindsight, perhaps the most pervasive feeling one has is that during the deceptions practised upon the policeman he is forced to function as something more than the virgin doomed to die. His presence for the two days before the May Day festival has a dual purpose; to integrate him symbolically into a community which is alien to him but simultaneously to highlight the islanders' own carnivalesque mood, from the *anteludia* (preliminary rituals before the festival proper) to their dreadful sacrifice. However serious the purpose of his enticement to Summerisle, the dialogue and interaction Howie conducts with the community highlights an interesting irony; namely, that he is living in a Presbyterian past while they are apparently more in tune with 1970s sexual and religious liberalism. This is an *hors texte* reading which audiences at the time, brought up on this style of crude comic horseplay, may have brought to the film.

Even so, such cinematic 'Carry On' capers would be a surprising find on a remote Scottish island and it is perhaps wiser to assume that Summerisle is in Saturnalian mood and mode. The question is: are they exaggerating the licentiousness to make a statement about carnival time and to force Howie into playing Lent before he plays Licence (the figure represented by Punch)?[12] We could view Howie as the upright figure of austerity necessary to intensify the spirit of carnival in the Summerisle *monde renversé*, where excess and misrule are legitimised for the period of celebration. Howie is not just the butt but also the facilitator of the comedy. All his pained surprise, disapproving moral stances and entrapment into bacchanal accentuates the feeling of festival time for the islanders. The creators of this dialectical tension, Hardy and Shaffer, may not have

---

[12]   This tension between release and restraint is the focus of Bristol's chapter on the festive *agon* in *Carnival and Theater*.

had a Bakhtinian dimension in mind for Howie's persona but they are expecting their audience to laugh at Howie's shocked responses to the Summerisle situation. The horror of the final sacrifice scene is intensified by a first time viewer's recollection of these apparently lighter moments during the film.[13]

The most fascinating orchestration of the policeman's appropriately sacrificial behaviour comes towards the end of the film when Howie is compelled to take on an heroic and isolated role as saviour of the child he believes is to be sacrificed on May Day. In his detailed and determined search for the missing Rowan, Howie turns the village upside down and enters every house and shop. This is a more prolonged sequence in the restored version of the film and the musical score accentuates the playfulness of the locals in directing the policeman's fruitless search. Of his own free will, and with remarkable thoroughness, he conducts a *lustrum*, a religious round of Summerisle, purifying every dwelling with his clumsy and intrusive presence, before joining the procession to the sea, suitably disguised (in both senses) as Punch. This procession continues its cathartic circuit around the boundaries of the village and through the fields to the appointed place of sacrifice.

The ritual is seen through to the end, relentless and pitiless. With uncertain and halting steps (he just cannot cut capers) Howie has been fooled into playing the part of Punch willingly, almost to the end. Christopher Lee amused the cast of the film by ad-libbing his line 'Shake your bladder' as he urged Howie/Punch to play the game with some panache. Of course, Lee's character, Lord Summerisle,

---

[13]   The move from unrestrained enjoyment (especially of sex) to sacrifices of a more serious nature can be paralleled with the Roman games held in honour of Flora, which lasted from 28 April to 3 May by the time of the emperor Augustus. The Floralia shows were held in the Circus Maximus and included the showering of spectators with fertility related vetches, beans and lupines. Striptease plays formed part of the entertainment, which might lead us to think that Willow's naked dance has a Roman ritualistic model. In Roman times the month of May was full of gloomy observances and festivals to appease the dead spirits. See Ogilvie, *The Romans and Their Gods in the Age of Augustus*, pp. 82-85.

is fully aware that Howie, not MacGregor, is under the costume. His chiding only accentuates the awkward and inhibited actions of the reluctant reveller. The mask and costume cannot compensate for Howie's body-language as it has none of the physical looseness such a festive sacrifice demands. Howie still wears the policeman's uniform underneath, embodying the lawful, the Lenten, under the licentious and anarchic. Howie's demeanour, both his physical posture and his psychological state, demonstrates how 'knotted up' he is.[14] Howie is disrobed of his Punch and policeman guises and forcibly dressed in the loose clothing appropriate for a sacrificial victim, the absence of knots being essential for any efficacious magical or supernatural ceremony.[15]

Once the awful truth of his situation is revealed, Howie struggles to escape. His resistance is ill-omened: in Roman rituals the chosen animal had to be replaced if it attempted to flee or did not approach the altar of its own accord. Animals were induced to bob their heads as if in agreement with their fate and in harmony with the community. Meuli identifies this artificial and superficial consent as an aspect of the 'comedy of innocence' which releases the community from responsibility for the slaughter.[16] Howie's *lustral* engagement with so many residents of Summerisle has also invested the community with collective responsibility; the comedy of innocence is a process that absolves each individual of the blood guilt the slaughter of the victim entails.

As Burkert observes, 'human sacrifice is a possibility that, as a horrible threat, stands behind every sacrifice.'[17] Howie's bull-like

---

[14]   In the feature length commentary recorded December 2001 (moderated by Mark Kermode and included in the Studio Canal DVD, *The Wicker Man: The Director's Cut*) Edward Woodward explains that he had chosen a tight fitting size for his policeman's uniform so that he could express constraint and awkwardness in his body language.

[15]   'A peculiarity of magic is its fear of knots: every knot represents a binding, and may therefore carry a counteractive force.' See McCreight, 'Sacrificial Ritual in Apuleius' *Metamorphoses*', p. 47.

[16]   Meuli, 'Greichische Opferbräuche', pp. 224-26.

[17]   Burkert, *Savage Energies*, p. 14.

bellowing further fudges the boundaries between animal and human victim. His desperate descant singing of the psalm, *The Lord is my Shepherd,* replays with due distortion the earlier Christian church service that the restored version of the film (and the American theatrical release of the 1990s) retrieved from the cutting room floor.[18] The contrast is painful as Howie had been safe and secure in the bosom of his church and had preached confidently from the pulpit in this opening scene. At the moment of his martyr's death on the Pagan island, Howie looks down in despair upon an equally attentive religious congregation. Such a distressed sacrificial victim would not have been considered a good omen in Greco-Roman festivals. Howie is an ultimately suspect and contrived offering to the gods. However, the film has such a dreadful closure that the uncertain future for Summerisle and its apples is not likely to be foregrounded for the first time viewer.

The community reaffirms itself in cheery singing. This could be interpreted as a culminating moment of social solidarity and a chronological and cultural re-integration with a past that never really existed. Habinek suggests that scapegoat festivals are a strategy for the community to re-establish its internal harmony, to differentiate its own civic identity from the world beyond its boundaries.[19] The Summerisle community has rejected selecting any one of its own number as a sacrifice, hence Howie's own honorary status among them and his promotion to king for May time. We have heard from Lord Summerisle that animals have only limited acceptability as offerings to the gods.

As the wicker cage containing its victims falls on the cliffs of Summerisle, the chorus, with its childlike swaying (like a Greek choral strophe and antistrophe), is dwarfed in sound and size by a telling tragic score, a haunting brass solo which stands out from

---

[18] In his conference contribution, the film's associate music director, Gary Carpenter, noted that Edward Woodward extemporised through this scene, which was disturbing, even frightening, to enact. The descant version of the hymn was a spontaneous outburst on Woodward's part.

[19] Habinek, 'Lucius' Rite of Passage', p. 54.

the crashing of the sea and the crackling of the sacrificial flames. The last cries of Howie merge into the striking of the final chords. The lone instrument functions as a funereal coda and perhaps casts doubt on the survival of the community, however oblivious they are to the horror of their crime. The murderous collective is submerged in the fiery horizon, a Pagan patchwork that disappears beneath the setting sun.

The Summerisle community seems indivisible to the very end, but the lord has been momentarily shaken by Howie's prediction of the ruler's fate: only the death of the true king will be sufficient to appease the gods if crop strains fail again next year. Burkert writes: 'All participate but one stands at their head – The same expression "thuesthai" means to sacrifice on one's own behalf and to be sacrificed. Sacrificer and victim are so correlated as to be nearly identified. Self asserting life presupposes death'.[20] Burkert's statement finds realisation in Howie's prophecy; this is the meeting of the classical concept of sacrifice with the sacrificed victim's spontaneous reading of the situation. A sequel to *The Wicker Man* ought to start with the slaughter of Lord Summerisle as he is Howie's ritualistic reflection, as well as his antagonist.

Bibliography

Bahktin, M., *Problems of Dostoevsky's Poetics*, trans. R. W. Rotsel (Ann Arbor, Michigan: Ardis, 1973).

Bremmer, J., 'Scapegoat Rituals in Ancient Greece', *Harvard Studies in Classical Philology*, 87 (1983), pp. 299-320.

Bristol, M., *Carnival and Theater: Plebeian culture and the structure of authority in Renaissance England* (London, New York: Routledge, 1989).

Burkert, W., *Savage Energies: Lessons of myth and ritual in*

---

[20] Burkert, *Savage Energies*, p. 15. Rigby, in his screen history of Christopher Lee, p. 154, notes that as Summerisle, Lee 'betrays a flicker of anxiety when Howie defiantly nominates him as next year's sacrifice.'

ancient Greece (Chicago and London: University of Chicago Press, 2001).

Habinek. T. N., 'Lucius' Rite of Passage', *Materiale e Discusione*, 25 (1990), pp. 49-66.

Hardy, R. (Director), *The Wicker Man – Special Edition Director's Cut* (Canal+, [1973] 2002).

Hardy, R. and Shaffer, A., *The Wicker Man*, 3rd ed (London: Pan Books, 2000).

James, P., *Unity in Diversity: A Study of Apuleius'* Metamorphoses (Hildesheim: Olms-Weidmann, 1987).

McCreight, T. D., 'Sacrificial Ritual in Apuleius' *Metamorphoses*', *Groningen Colloquia on the Novel*, 5, (1993), pp. 31-62.

Mueli, K., 'Greichische Opferbräuche' in *Phyllobolia für Peter von der Mühll*, ed. by O. Gigon (Basel: Benno Schwabe and Co., 1946), pp. 185-288.

Ogilvie, R. M., *The Romans and Their Gods in the Age of Augustus (Ancient Culture and Society)* (London: Chatto and Windus, 1974).

Rigby, J., *Christopher Lee: The authorised screen history* (London: Reynolds and Hearn, 2001).

Rives, J., 'Human Sacrifice among Pagans and Christians', *The Journal of Roman Studies*, 85 (1995), pp. 65-85.

Wiseman, T. P., 'The Publication of *De Bello Gallico*' in *Julius Caesar as Artful Reporter: The war commentaries as political instruments*, ed. K. Welch and A. Powell (London: Duckworth, 1998), pp. 1-9.

Sacrifice, Society and Religion in *The Wicker Man*

Luc Racaut

The Wicker Man is an ambiguous film. I would argue that it is this
very ambiguity that explains why it is still debated today while so
many other films of its day have been forgotten. The film's primary
value is in depicting in vivid strokes the stark contrast between
modernity/civilisation and pre-modernity/barbarism. As such, it
seems appropriate for an historian to intervene to place the film in
a wider debate about civilisation, where religion and law play a
central role. Indeed, religion and law are both very prominent themes
in the film, embodied in the flesh by Lord Summerisle and Sergeant
Howie. Both are archetypal figures of authority, one representing
law (Howie) and the other religion (Summerisle), although the two
tropes are intermingled (Summerisle is the lord of the island while
Howie is clearly religious). This ambiguity is at the very heart of
what distinguishes the 'modern' from the 'pre-modern' in classical
(meaning eighteenth century) understanding: in a pre-modern society,
religion and law are indistinguishable, while in modern 'enlightened'
times these are identified respectively with a separate church and
state. In the film, Summerisle, the charismatic leader, is both high
priest and judge of the island, while Howie has a public persona (the
policeman) distinct from his more private self (the Christian whom
we see take communion in the director's cut of the film). *The Wicker
Man* offers a critique of this dichotomy between modern and pre-
modern, in showing the connections between two interpretations of
sacrifice that we have inherited from Enlightenment historiography.
These require an historical explanation.

Sacrifice was indeed the centrepiece of the film; according to

the words of its director, Robin Hardy: 'we have striven to show how sacrifice works.'[1] And that it has done remarkably well, in more eloquent terms than James George Frazer or Emile Durkheim, or any other anthropologist from whose work *The Wicker Man* clearly borrows.[2] It does so by using tropes (carnival, the witches' Sabbath, burnings at the stake) from popular imagination, which still have resonance today in what I have no choice but to call 'collective memory'. This, in fact, is the very argument of the film: that underneath a thin veneer of civility lie the still glowing embers of the 'old ways', which need only a small spark to start blazing again. This was a countercultural idea popular at the time of the film's inception that has since fallen out of favour. Beyond this countercultural context, which alone does not explain the enduring appeal of the film, lies a much more valuable and lasting critique of modernity. It is this post-modern critique which I will briefly outline insofar as it bears relation to the film.

Pre-Christian practices

A few years before the comic strip (and later film) character Judge Dredd uttered the words 'I am the law' for the first time, Sergeant Howie could be seen to be at once the arm, the judge, and the executor of the law. On the remote island of Summerisle he is the sole member of 'Her Majesty's Constabulary', to paraphrase Howie himself. In other words, he embodies modernity, decency, a clear sense of moral duty and courage. In any other context, Howie would be the hero, but he is also a virgin, an overwrought point in the film, and a fool, whose garb he dons during the sacrificial procession. He is a devout Christian, whom we see praying when tempted by Willow in one of the film's most memorable scenes, and is appalled by the unbridled sexuality of the islanders and their irreligious ways. In this regard he is ridiculed by the islanders and set up as an unwittingly

---

[1]   See the director's commentary on the Director's Cut version of *The Wicker Man* DVD.

[2]   Durkheim, *Les Formes Elémentaires de la Vie Religieuse*.

comic character. He is also an anti-hero, for whom the audience cannot help but exhibit sympathy. In the words of Lord Summerisle, he is the perfect sacrifice, and he is indeed burnt in the wicker man at the end in a roaring climax of fire, song and horror. The film is a fairly straightforward re-enactment of pre-Christian practices, Sergeant Howie being the archetypal scapegoat, improbably encapsulating all the attributes listed in Frazer's *The Golden Bough*.[3] We are appalled by the sacrifice and this reaction is the very backbone of many horror films: they build on existing dominant values, and are, in this respect, deeply conservative and, one could argue, reactionary. The 'frisson' of horror films derives from a tempting peek into the world of unlicensed sex and violence where customary conventions of decency are temporarily suspended, but are re-imposed at the end of the film. *The Wicker Man*, however, is exceptional in deconstructing the very mechanism on which its own appeal rests, in borrowing the age-old device of 'the play within the play'. On numerous occasions during the film, sacrifice is hinted at, in drawings and representations (for instance, the recurring topos of bread being baked in the shape of a person, hinting at cannibalism), as if the director wanted to announce to the audience that the film's climactic sacrifice was a pretence, thus dulling its impact. In this sense, it is suffused with irony.

The film is indeed satirical or ironic in many places. For example, the presentation of Lord Summerisle's character is best regarded as self-consciously tongue-in-cheek (a tribute to Hardy's knowing casting and direction of Christopher Lee). There are other indications in the film that what we are witnessing is not to be taken literally and, indeed, stands for something else. This is reflected in the film's deployment of the principle of analogy. The maypole represents an erect virile member, a hare is placed in the coffin instead of Rowan's body, a frog is used to remove a small child's cough, and effigies of children are baked in the shape of cakes, in a classic representation of the principle of substitution of one thing for another. Like Howie, the spectator is fooled by the display of the islanders into

---

[3] See Koven, 'The Folklore Fallacy', in this volume.

believing that Rowan is indeed going to be sacrificed in order to replenish the crops, and in a last minute U-turn we realise, again with Howie, that he is going to be sacrificed in her stead. Again this is an unproblematic representation of the mechanism of scapegoating described in Frazer's *The Golden Bough* with reference to human and animal sacrifice in numerous pre-modern societies.

This is where the film is unlike any other horror film of its genre: it denounces the very mechanism that usually lies hidden, that fools us into believing that a sacrifice has taken place. By exposing what the islanders are doing through the archetypical last minute speech by Lord Summerisle (himself the classic villain), *The Wicker Man* introduces a final twist which renders the sacrifice all the more appalling by denying it any efficacy. When, in normal circumstances, we would derive a sense of cathartic liberation in witnessing (with the islanders) the death of the Janus-like figure of the fool, our sympathies are clearly drawn towards the innocent victim whose pathetic end we are forced to witness. It calls up, deliberately or not, the images of public executions, burnings at the stake and scenes of torture that litter the history of Western culture, and, of course, the crucifixion of Christ, explicitly invoked by both Howie and Summerisle. It is Summerisle who confers upon Howie the status of martyr, incompatible with the original premise of the sacrifice and the scapegoat.

Human Sacrifice and the Early Modern Church

Anthropology teaches that the nature of sacrifice is precisely the ability to believe that something can take the place of something else on the altar. Leviticus instructs that a goat can be sacrificed 'as a sin offering' and the expression 'scapegoat' comes from Leviticus 16:22: 'the goat shall bear on itself all their iniquities to a barren region.' The scapegoat is by definition innocent, and is sacrificed in atonement for the sins of the community, thus ridding the community of its guilt. Frazer has catalogued many other examples of this ancient practice, where the victim is sometimes animal, sometimes human, and where its remains are in several cases eaten or burnt

(or both). The Old Testament itself denounces the practice of the Babylonians, who ritually burnt children in sacrifice to their god Molech.[4] To ritually slaughter an animal was far preferable to sacrificing a human being in a culture that saw killing people as a cardinal sin. The process by which animal sacrifice was substituted for human sacrifice is epitomised in the story of Isaac and Abraham in Genesis 22. This principle of substitution of one victim for another suffuses Judeo-Christian culture and indeed was transmitted to Christianity via the New Testament's account of the last supper and the crucifixion. Christ is called the 'paschal lamb', named after the burnt offering in the Jewish ceremony of Passover, and is transformed into the central sacrament of the Eucharist through the institution of the Last Supper. This points to another form of sacrifice: that of the host that we see Howie receive in the celebration of the Eucharist during a flashback in the famous bedchamber scene.[5] So a victim is substituted for another, in a way that the islanders understand but Howie does not. Rowan's mother says to Howie in the film: 'you do not understand the true nature of sacrifice.' Indeed, it is ironic on several levels, most obviously because Howie himself will be substituted for Rowan as a sacrificial victim, but also more subtly because he does not understand the sacrificial nature of his own religious practice.

In a clear teleological progression from barbarism to civilisation, the Eucharist represents the culmination of the process of substitution, the bread and the wine standing for the flesh and blood of Christ. Christ himself fulfilled all the requirements for the perfect sacrifice, and the New Testament establishes the crucifixion's sacrificial nature. Frazer significantly ends his in-depth study of the scapegoat, in the third book of *The Golden Bough*, with a chapter on the crucifixion.

The film deliberately conflates varieties of sacrificial practice: human, animal and symbolic. In juxtaposing the Christian sacrifice

---

[4]   NRSV, Leviticus 18:21, 20:2, 20:3, 20:4; 2 Kings 23:10; Jeremiah 19:5, 32:35.
[5]   Cavanaugh, 'Eucharistic Sacrifice and the Social Imagination in Early Modern Europe', p. 589.

of the Eucharist with the Pagan practice of human and animal offerings, *The Wicker Man* points to the similarities between the two, and the absurdity of both Summerisle's and Howie's respective faiths. Lord Summerisle bestows on Howie (and Howie in turn adopts) the role of the martyr. Howie stoically bears his fate, perishing with hymns stuck in his throat. Thus, the film's ending demonstrates the co-dependence of Pagan and Christian sacrifice, and thereby constitutes a critique of the efficacy of the sacrifice of Christ on the cross, its re-enactment in the Eucharist and the death of martyrs.

The film's treatment of sacrifice draws on a characteristically Protestant (Howie is supposed to be an Episcopalian) line of argument that goes as far back as the Wars of Religion themselves (1562-1598). Indeed this period of Europe's history (more than the pre-Christian era it seems) is replete with stories of orgies, human sacrifice, even cannibalism, and, of course, burnings and martyrs. Also central to this period is the critique of the sacrifice of the Mass as a substitute for the real life sacrifice of Christ on the Cross, a debate that was responsible for more bloodshed than was represented in all the Hammer films combined.

The debate over the nature of the Eucharist merits further remarks. First of all, there was a genuine disgust, often expressed in extremely vitriolic terms by evangelicals, at the 'sacrificial' reading of the gospels. In response, Catholics often used the word 'meat' to describe the host, in order to hammer home their defence of transubstantiation. The theology of the most prolific French writer of Catholic devotion in this period, René Benoist, seems here particularly relevant to the debate about the substitution of a bloodless sacrifice for a bloody one:[6]

> I sacrifice every day to the almighty God, who is true and alive: not the flesh of bulls, nor the blood of goats: but I sacrifice the immaculate lamb, on the altar of the cross where he was immolated: the sacrificial lamb that remains whole and alive after everyone has eaten its flesh, and drunken its blood. I profess that

---

[6]   The expression 'bloodless sacrifice' is used in Backus, *Guillaume Postel et Jean Boulaese*, p. 13.

he is truly sacrificed, his flesh is truly eaten and his blood drank
by the people [. . .] But when he is eaten he is not cut up [...] in
the way meat would be by a butcher [. . .] but he is received whole
and without wounds [. . .] like the flesh of the angels.[7]

This proved to be the most divisive issue amongst Christians on all
sides of the multi-faceted confessional debate. The denunciation of
the carnality of the sacrifice of the mass was expressed in a number
of ways, notably through comparisons with real life cannibals that
evangelicals first came across in Brazil in the mid-sixteenth century.[8]

These dramatic images resonated with nightmares of human
sacrifice, orgies, infanticide and cannibalism that colonised the
medieval and early modern imagination. In some instances these
nightmares become flesh and were acted upon. Conspiracy theories
were often targeted at minority groups that were, in turn, sacrificed
on the altar of collective hysteria. Of course Jews figure prominently
in the family tree of infamy, as do witches and lepers and, perhaps
less famously, heretics.[9]

The 'blood libel', the drinking and eating of a slain infant's flesh,
itself a mockery of Passover and the Last Supper, first emerged during
the Roman persecution of Jews and Christians. After the conversion
of Constantine, when Christianity became the official religion of the
Empire, this story was appropriated by the Church Fathers, who
used it against the first Christian heretics; Epiphanius of Salamis
(315-403) employed it against the Gnostics:

In the first place, they hold their wives in common [. . .] the next
thing they do is feast [. . .] they next go crazy for each other [. . .] And
when the wretched couple has made love [. . .] the woman becomes
pregnant [. . .] They extract the fetus at the stage appropriate for

---

[7] Benoist, *Claire Probation de la Necessaire Manducation*, sigs E2r, F3r-v,
     G2r, G3v, G4v, H1r, H3r, K2r.

[8] Lestringan, *Une Sainte Horreur ou le Voyage en Eucharistie* XVIe-XVIIIe
     Siècle.

[9] Ginzburg, *Ecstasies: Deciphering the Witches' Sabbath*, p. 33, p. 36, pp.
     38-9; Racaut, 'Accusations of Infanticide on the Eve of the French Wars of
     Religion', pp. 18-34.

their enterprise, take this aborted infant, and cut it up in a trough shaped like a pestle. And they mix honey, pepper, and certain other perfumes and spices [. . .] and then all the revellers [. . .] assemble, and each eats a piece of the child with his fingers.[10]

There are many variations on this story; sometimes the child is torn to pieces, burnt and baked into a cake, covered by a mound of flour or pricked to death with needles. The tale was used against a variety of groups ranging from Jews to Templars and, in the sixteenth century, Protestants. But unlike their predecessors in infamy, the Protestants had read the scriptures and the Church Fathers were able to reiterate the defence against the blood libel that had first been erected by Tertullian.[11] The latter had argued that these accusations were groundless and that in fact the persecution of Christians entitled them to the status of martyrs, on whose blood the Church would be founded. The public torture of heretics, in Roman and in early modern times, reflected the torturing of Christ on the cross and the victims were thereby elevated to the status of martyrs, literally 'witnesses of the truth.' Thus the status of martyr that Lord Summerisle confers upon Howie before his incineration inside the wicker cage gives Christianity a pyrrhic victory over Paganism. The final scene of The Wicker Man is therefore a very vivid re-enact-ment of the Christian and Protestant denunciation of the sacrificial mechanism and the hypocrisy of the very institution that perpetuated it in history: the Church.[12] In the sixteenth century, Reformers exposed the contradictions in the historical Church that the film describes, maybe not for the first time, but with such force that the Church never recovered from it.

---

[10] Williams, *The Panarion of Epiphanius of Salamis*, Vol I, pp. 85-87. There are many other versions of this story; amongst others, Müller, *The De Haeresibus of Saint Augustine*, p. 74; Labande, *Guibert de Nogent*, pp. 430-31.

[11] Glover and Rendall, *Tertullian*; Racaut, 'Religious Polemic and Huguenot Self-Perception and Identity, 1554-1619', pp. 29-43.

[12] Girard, *Things Hidden Since the Foundation of the World*, pp. 126-30, pp. 250-51.

Secular Law and Sacrifice

Although the director of *The Wicker Man* announced that his intention had been to create an anti-religious film, I feel that it would be too simplistic to sum it up in this way.[13] The film also offers an implicit critique of the law, in putting side by side the mechanism of scapegoating and Howie's own self-righteous crusade. One reading of *The Wicker Man* suggests that Howie comes to Summerisle looking for a culprit, a guilty party, the murderer of Rowan Morrison, who can be arrested and sacrificed on the altar of judicial retribution. The film plays on the theme of the scapegoat, first by introducing the idea of a missing child, often at the origin of moral panics in the Middle Ages, which culminated, as we have seen, in religious violence. Interestingly, Howie is looking for just the sort of practices that minority groups were accused of in the medieval and early modern periods: orgies, ritual murder and sacrifice, cannibalism and infanticide.[14] Indeed he asks Rowan Morrison's mother: 'what kind of mother are you that can stand by and see your own child slaughtered?', a question which was used by Erasmus himself against the evangelicals.[15] This indicates that the law has a tendency to typecast culprits in the same way that scapegoats were selected in the medieval period.

The law, in a modernist narrative, substituted itself for mob violence and offered, in public executions, the spectacle of expiation of the condemned, in a cathartic spectacle that replaced the public burning at the stake of heretics or witches. In a pre-modern society, executions served a didactic function where the elite appealed to

---

[13] Hardy stated this in his contribution to '*The Wicker Man*: Rituals, Readings and Reactions' conference, University of Glasgow, Crichton Campus, 14-15 July 2003.

[14] Langmuir, 'Thomas of Monmouth', pp. 820-46; Langmuir, 'The Knight's Tale of Young Hugh of Lincoln', pp. 459-82.

[15] Erasmus, *Liber de Sarcienda Ecclesiae Concordia Deque Sedandis Opinionum Dissidiis*, reproduced in Dolan, *The Essential Erasmus*, pp. 442-43; Lalanne, *Journal d'un Bourgeois de Paris sous le Règne de François Premier*, p. 429.

the audience's consensus values. However, the standards of the dominant elite became threatened when the masses began to be appalled rather than awed by the spectacle of pain and death. The intended pedagogic instruction, as we have seen, was subverted by Protestants who claimed the status of martyrs for the victims of religious persecution, transferring the infamy of the victims onto the executioners.

As the 'theatre of execution' gave way to the 'theatre of martyrdom' the authorities reacted, notably in France, by sentencing heretics to be hanged for sedition rather than burned for heresy.[16] This had two consequences: first, Protestants could no longer turn the spectacle of suffering into a sign of election, and second, the mob was denied its cathartic spectacle of the scapegoat suffering at the stake. The populace, which had flocked to these executions, was disappointed and soon wanted to take matters into its own hands. The people attacked the sergeants and vented their anger on the supplicants themselves, often hacking them to pieces in a parody of the quartering that was reserved for the most grievous crimes (parricide and treason). This was generalised in the massacres (a word itself derived from butchery) that litter the entire period of the Religious Wars, especially in the intermediate periods of peace when Protestantism was officially tolerated by royal edicts. In killing Protestants indiscriminately, the Catholic mob expressed their contempt for the laws of the kingdom that tolerated the presence of the unthinkable in their midst.[17] The massacre of St Bartholomew's Day on 14 August 1572 saw thousands of Protestants killed in the streets of Paris, sometimes by their own neighbours. It has been argued that the parallel plot to decapitate the Protestant hierarchy was an attempt by the Crown to reclaim a certain degree of legitimacy by embracing the violence of its subjects.[18]

This failed and provoked the rebellion of an increasing proportion of France's Catholic subjects. They eventually turned against

---

[16] Nicholls, 'The Theatre of Martyrdom in the French Reformation', pp. 49-73.

[17] Racaut, *Hatred in Print*, pp. 23-37.

[18] Crouzet, *La Nuit de la Saint-Barthélemy*, pp. 530-31.

King Henri III, who was assassinated in 1589. In one of his final lines, Howie tells the islanders that if the sacrifice fails to restore the harvest, then they will turn on Lord Summerisle next. The parallel between the position of Henri III and the threat to Lord Summerisle is clear: the king failed to channel the destructive violence of the mob against the Protestants and paid the price.

It was the rule of law, established by the intervention of Henri IV, that re-established concord, if only temporarily, and paved the way for the Bourbons' consolidation of royal power in the seventeenth century. The rule of law, the end to all non-state sanctioned violence through the exercise of a force unmatched by anything that the subjects could muster, put an end to the Wars of Religion. But sacrifice did not altogether vanish, as the public executions of criminals became more and more elaborate until the State was sufficiently powerful to no longer require these outward demonstrations of force. At some point in the eighteenth century, according to Michel Foucault, the public display of suffering became counter productive and the State resorted to the internalisation of violence in the institution of the prison.[19] One interpretation of the film is that it offers a critique of the substitution of the rule of law, represented by Howie, by the sacrificial mechanism of pre-modern societies, exposing the similarities between the self-serving processes of the secular judicial system and the way in which a sacrificial victim is chosen within Paganism.

As I said at the beginning, Lord Summerisle stands for religion whereas Sergeant Howie represents the law. At one point, Summerisle says to Howie: 'we don't commit murder here, we're a deeply religious people.' The implication is that the concept of 'murder' is anachronistic in the context of the religious ritual that the islanders are trying to recreate. At the end of the film, Howie briefly embraces the role of martyr, conferred upon him by Summerisle, but ultimately falls back on his public persona of policeman when he cries out: 'You can wrap it up any way you like, but you are about to commit murder.' Are the concept of 'murder' and the legal definition of

---

19   Foucault, *Surveiller et Punir*.

interpersonal violence vindicated in the film? Given that Howie has the final line, this would seem to be the case. But I think it would do *The Wicker Man* an injustice to conclude that it has any single interpretation. Amongst the film's remarkable features are its challenge of received wisdom about religion, modernity and the meaning of sacrifice, and the manner in which it opens a debate that has no easy resolution.

Bibliography

Backus, I., ed., *Guillaume Postel et Jean Boulaese: De summopere et le miracle de Laon, 1566* (Geneva: Droz, 1995).

Benoist, R., *Claire Probation de la necessaire manducation de la substantielle & reale humanité de Jesus Christ, vray Dieu & vray homme, au S. Sacrement de l'autel* (Paris: Nicolas Chesneau, 1561).

Cavanaugh, W. T., 'Eucharistic Sacrifice and the Social Imagination in Early Modern Europe', *Journal of Medieval and Early Modern Studies*, 31, 3 (2001), pp. 585-605.

Crouzet, D., *La Nuit de la Saint-Barthélemy: Un rêve perdu de la Renaissance* (Paris: Fayard, 1994).

Dolan, J. P., *The Essential Erasmus* (New York: New American Library, 1964).

Durkheim, J. E., *Les Formes Elémentaires de la Vie Religieuse* (Paris: Presses Universitaires de France, 1994).

Erasmus, D., *Liber de Sarcienda Ecclesiae Concordia Deque Sedandis Opinionum Dissidiis* (Basel: J. Froben, 1533).

Foucault, M., *Discipline and Punish: The birth of the prison* (London: Penguin, 1991).

Ginzburg, C., *Ecstasies: Deciphering the witches' Sabbath* (London: Penguin, 1991).

Girard, R., *Things Hidden Since the Foundation of the World* (Palo Alto: Stanford University Press, 1994).

Glover, T. R. and Rendall, G. H., eds., *Tertullian: Apology* (London: Heinemann, 1984).

Greengrass, M., 'Hidden Transcripts: Secret histories and personal testimonies of religious violence in the French wars of religion', *The Massacre in History*, ed. M. Levene and P. Roberts (Oxford: Oxford University Press, 1999).

Gregory, B. S., *Salvation at Stake: Christian martyrdom in early modern Europe* (London: Harvard University Press, 1999).

Hardy, R. (Director), *The Wicker Man – Special Edition Director's Cut* (Canal+, [1973] 2002).

Koven, M., 'The Folklore Fallacy: A folkloristic/filmic perspective on *The Wicker Man*', *The Quest for the Wicker Man*, ed. B. Franks, S. Harper, J. Murray and L. Stevenson (Edinburgh: Luath, 2005).

Labande, E. R., ed., *Guibert de Nogent: Autobiographie* (Paris: Les Belles Lettres, 1981).

Lalanne, L. ed., *Journal d'un Bourgeois de Paris sous le Règne de François Premier (1515-1536)*, (Paris: J. Renouard, 1854).

Langmuir, G., 'The Knight's Tale of Young Hugh of Lincoln', *Speculum*, 47 (1972), pp. 459-482.

_____, 'Thomas of Monmouth: Detector of Ritual Murder', *Speculum*, 59 (1984), pp. 820-846.

Lestringant, F. *Une Sainte Horreur ou le Voyage en Eucharistie XVIe-XVIIIe Siècle* (Paris: Presses Universitaires de France, 1996).

Merback, M. B., *The Thief, the Cross and the Wheel: Pain and the spectacle of punishment in Medieval and Renaissance Europe* (London: Reaktion, 1999).

Monter, W., *Judging the French Reformation: Heresy trials by sixteenth-century parlements* (London: Harvard University Press, 1999).

Müller, L. G., ed., *The De Haeresibus of Saint Augustine: A translation with an introduction and commentary* (Washington: Catholic University of America Press, 1956).

Nicholls, D., 'The Theatre of Martyrdom in the French Reformation', *Past & Present*, 121 (1988), pp. 49-73.

Racaut, L., 'Religious Polemic and Huguenot Self-Perception and Identity, 1554-1619', *Society and Culture in the Huguenot World, 1559-1685*, ed. R. Mentzer and A. Spicer (Cambridge: Cambridge University Press, 2001), pp. 29-43.

_____, 'Accusations of Infanticide on the Eve of the French Wars of Religion', *Infanticide: Historical perspectives on child murder and concealment, 1550-2000*, ed. M. Jackson (Aldershot: Ashgate, 2002).

_____, *Hatred in Print: Catholic propaganda and Protestant identity during the French wars of religion* (Aldershot: Ashgate, 2002).

White, H., *Metahistory: The historical imagination in nineteenth-century Europe* (London: The Johns Hopkins University Press, 1973).

Williams, F., ed., *The Panarion of Epiphanius of Salamis* (2 vols, Leiden: E. J. Brill, 1987-1994).

Anthropological Investigations: An innocent exploration of *The Wicker Man* culture

Donald V. L. Macleod

Introduction

THE PRINCIPAL AIMS of this chapter are to show that *The Wicker Man* might be concluded to be an 'ethnographic' film, and as such, how the film reveals the horror of our own, western, society. It is the investigation of Summerisle's 'culture' that reveals this for the audience. Sergeant Howie, the protagonist of the film, is treated, from this perspective, as a type of investigating researcher, in the mould of an anthropologist. For the purposes of this chapter I use the term 'anthropology', and by extension 'anthropologists', to refer to the disciplines and practitioners of both social and cultural anthropology as practised in Europe and the Americas. Howie is, thus, regarded as a representative of his own culture and by extension, a model of the mainstream western audience for the film. Furthermore, he is understood as the personification of the more limiting and negative aspects of western cultural values, these being narrow-mindedness, intolerance, violence and bigotry.

The Meaning of Ethnographic Film

Firstly, we should investigate ethnographic film; its goals, characteristics and development. Generally speaking it seeks to document a culture and tradition, largely for educational purpose; although entertainment is occasionally an aim. We must also bear in mind that one of the original intentions of the anthropological project

was to allow western observers to reach insights into their own culture through learning about others. As the nineteenth century researcher Edward Tylor explained: 'There seems to be no human thought so primitive as to have lost its bearing on our own thought, nor so ancient as to have broken its connection with our own life.'[1]

Some of the earliest films regarded by scholars as ethnographic material were documentaries of expeditions: for example the explorer Alfred Haddon going to the Torres Straits in 1898. Another recorded exploratory journey follows the progress of gold prospectors in the early twentieth century who come across hitherto unencountered groups in the New Guinea Highlands – and it includes the astounded reaction of both groups to one another. This was a somewhat picaresque adventure, highlighting differences in technological ability and emphasising the apparent 'primitiveness' of the indigenous people through such comparisons. Many years later, the prospectors returned and recorded their journey, and showed the earlier, first film to the villagers – provoking hilarious reactions from them. It was an occasion that, ostensibly, served to bond these people from radically different backgrounds. The return journey and the showing of the original footage, as portrayed in the film *First Contact* (1983), provide dramatic insights into cultural differences and transformations.

More famous and intentionally ethnographic is *Nanook of the North* (1922), which follows the hunting exploits and everyday activities of an Inuit and his family as he uses traditional equipment (kayak, igloo, spear and clothing) to go about his business. This film was an actual reconstruction of a disappearing lifestyle, orchestrated by the director (Robert Flaherty). Karl Heider, in his seminal book on ethnographic film, writes:

> Flaherty ventures into one of the more treacherous realms of ethnography. He created artifice to assert a truth [. . .]. In order to film Eskimo life inside an igloo, he had the Eskimo build an igloo set; it was a half-dome, twice life-size.[2]

---

[1]   Tylor, 1871, quoted in Lienhardt, *Social Anthropology*, p. 1.
[2]   Heider, *Ethnographic Film*, p. 22.

Similarly, Robert Gardner and John Marshalls' film *The Hunters* (1957), about the San people of Africa, used material filmed from many hunts to construct a single giraffe hunt, which formed the core of the film. This gave the impression of a single temporal episode, albeit somewhat disjointed. Nevertheless, the experience of the hunt, as well as the structure of a hunt, was successfully recreated.

In stark contrast to the above 'documentary' attempts, Gardner made films of ethnic groups in the 1960s and 70s which flirted with realism, used ethnographic references but transcended the genre in a manner reminiscent of symbolism; a move against the overt positivism of so many ethnographic works. He produced films strong in emotion and made subjective statements that continue to divide critics. Nevertheless, his work was grounded in ethnographic detail and focused on culturally specific activities. Here is Heider commenting on Gardner's film *The Nuer* (c.1971):

> It is one of the most visually beautiful films ever made, and it shows the rhythm and pace of Nuer life, which no ethnographer could ever capture in words. But the film is almost without ethnographic integrity. By this I mean that its principles are cinema aesthetic: its framing, cutting, and juxtaposition of images are done without regard for any ethnographic reality.[3]

He later goes on to qualify this position:

> But even if *The Nuer* is ethnographically unsound, it has real use in teaching anthropology. It can give students a general holistic feeling for the people, their cattle, and their environment, helping them to build a kind of cognitive landscape into which they can place Evans-Pritchard's written description of Nuer social organisation and ritual.[4]

These different styles of filmmaking indicate the powerful part that editing plays in the ethnographic film: it may be argued that these films become a constructed narrative oriented by the creator, although based on the subject's culture. Nichols points out the following:

---

[3]   Heider, *Ethnographic Film*, p. 35.
[4]   Heider, *Ethnographic Film*, p. 35.

First Contact does not tell us that the white gold-mining brothers who made first contact with the New Guinea Highland natives some fifty years ago have been and still are married to native women; *Nanook of the North* does not disclose the differences between its depiction of Eskimo life and the much more modern patterns of existence that Flaherty found but did not film.[5]

How to define an ethnographic film is therefore problematic. Heider suggests that ethnographic film is film which reflects ethnographic understanding, which he describes as: making a detailed description of human behaviour based on observation; relating specific observed behaviour to cultural norms; being holistic; things being understood in their social and cultural context; and having the goal of accuracy and truth (a philosophical problem).[6]

However, Heider admits that in many senses all films are ethnographic in that they are somehow about people; some clearly have ethnographic import without attempting the science of ethnography; these he calls 'Naïve Ethnographic Films'. Furthermore, he believes that the degree to which a film is ethnographic depends on the degree to which prior ethnographic understanding has informed the filmmaking.[7] Using these guidelines we can allow that *The Wicker Man* stands somewhere on the continuum between pure ethnographic film and Naïve Ethnographic Film, informed as it is by serious research, a point made clear by Tanya Krzywinska:

> The May Day festival is central to the dramatic events of *The Wicker Man*. This is a significant date in the Summerisle calendar, as it is the time allotted for fertility rites to ensure a good harvest. After a disastrous yield in the previous year, the inhabitants of Summerisle connive to offer the earth goddess a blood sacrifice to ensure fruitful abundance. It is preceded by a variety of celebratory rites drawn from the country practices documented by Frazer and the Folk-lore Society, and from Wiccan rites as informed by Murray and Gardner. They include dancing around

---

5   Nichols, *Ideology and the Image*, p. 124.
6   Heider, *Ethnographic Film*, pp. 5-8.
7   Heider, *Ethnographic Film*, p. 11.

a maypole, bawdy folk songs, mummery, sex outdoors, and jumping over fire.[8]

Peter Loizos, in his historical account of ethnographic film, tells us that they are a subset of documentary films more generally.[9] However, he refers to Nichols, who writes that: 'Documentaries, then, do not differ from fictions in their constructedness as texts, but in the representations they make. At the heart of documentary is less a story and its imaginary world than an argument about the historical world.'[10] Another commentator, Jay Ruby, proposed that ethnographic films should satisfy four criteria: be about whole cultures or definable portions; be informed by explicit or implicit theories of culture; be explicit about research and filming methods; and use a distinctively anthropological lexicon.[11] We are able to note that both Heider and Ruby require a significant input of anthropological research into an ethnographic film.

For the purposes of this chapter we should consider a film ethnographic if its central concern is with a culture and it adheres to one or more of the following guidelines: gives a genuine insight into the culture that we wish to examine; provides a genuine insight into our own culture; teaches us about the process of exploring another culture; and records a culture-specific activity. This is an open-ended way of including more work into the general class of ethnographic film and is not a limiting definition.

Sergeant Howie as the Fieldworker

The Wicker Man, as is well known, draws upon many details about 'exotic' cultures collected by anthropologists – in particular James G. Frazer, among others. It shares a number of qualities and preoccupations with anthropology, including an interest in ritual, cosmology, community, morality, interpretation, cultural relativity

---

8 Krzywinska, *A Skin for Dancing In*, p. 81.
9 Loizos, *Innovation in Ethnographic Film*, p. 5.
10 Nichols, *Ideology and the Image*, p. 111.
11 Jay Ruby, cited in Loizos, *Innovation in Ethnographic Film*, p. 9.

and sacrifice. We might imagine that *The Wicker Man* is an actual documentary, a 'reality' TV programme in which a policeman investigates an alternative community; all hidden lenses and hasty camerawork. But of course it was no such thing. Nevertheless, its camera work, cast and location remind us of grainy fly-on-the-wall documentaries: definitely not Hollywood. However, if all ethnographic films are constructions, with occasionally pre-designed storylines (the better to inform the audience about native rituals), then *The Wicker Man* instantiates a complex form of the deliberate construction of a 'culture'.

Sergeant Howie is an innocent investigator: innocent of the Summerislanders' way of life, and physically a virgin. He is new to the community and in this sense he is well suited as an anthropological fieldworker, who, ideally, according to many anthropological approaches, should be fresh to the culture, becoming like a child again – in the sense of being vulnerable, inexperienced and inquisitive. This innocence (so the theory goes) enables the fieldworker to experience that disorientation and momentary loss of home-support and corresponding cultural moorings, leading to a deeper immersion in the new culture, and therefore culminating in a fresh view of the society under scrutiny. This may seem paradoxical to the layman: moreover, it is often believed that the fieldworker should learn the language directly from the indigenous people afresh – often gaining their sympathy, support and trust.

Angela Cheater, when writing about anthropological fieldwork notes that:

> To demonstrate the interconnections among social institutions in a functional analysis requires deep and lengthy immersion in a working culture [. . .] More often, the anthropologist is in, but not of, that society, a privileged outsider even when participating in its social activity [. . .]
>
> Outsiders can ask questions, which would be inappropriate among locals; they can associate with almost anyone; they are expected to behave incomprehensibly to some degree.[12]

---

[12]   Cheater, *Social Anthropology*, pp. 38-39.

But Sergeant Howie differs markedly from our ideal anthropological fieldworker in that he has a very specific goal to achieve; he is not interested in the community as an academic exercise, has little sympathy with their views, and wants to escape and return home (well, maybe he is not so different). In fact, contrarily, Howie symbolises the 'anti-fieldworker' in these characteristics; furthermore, he blatantly represents the mainstream mainland establishment and society that will not tolerate deviance from its norms, interests and status quo. Cultural relativity, the ability to perceive the intrinsic worldview of another culture and to accept different 'ways of seeing' and behaving, so important to much of anthropology, does not form part of Howie's repertoire.

This inability to accept the 'other' culture's behaviour, coupled with a desperation to search for an answer to a problem, as well as a need to 'enter' the community, means that Howie acts as the perfect foil, emphasising their differences and highlighting their specificities. Ironically, he becomes, for the purposes of the ethnographic film, an excellent research device. And so, particular aspects of the culture become accentuated through their comparison with Howie's background and due to his strong reaction to them.

There is a Levi-Straussian structure[13] to the culture, with culturally defined oppositions leaping into the frame: frogs are placed in people's mouths, copulation occurs in graveyards, hares represent humans, sexual language enters the classroom. For Sergeant Howie, his world is in danger of being turned upside-down, and the final scene, with his own sacrifice as a virgin, becomes the ultimate surprise. Oppositions, of course, in these instances are cultural constructions, and these are regularly lampooned in the carnival event, a tradition in many Christian societies, an opportunity for role reversal, liminality and libidinous foolery. Taboos are relaxed in this period of social catharsis: 'certain adult play forms such as the pre-Lenten Carnival also act as a commentary on the 'real' world. They sanction insults and derision of authority figures, inversion of social

---

[13]   Levi-Strauss, *Structural Anthropology*.

status, clowning, parody, satire, and the like.'[14] The carnival-like procession towards the dramatic sacrificial end in *The Wicker Man* contains numerous figures that challenge conventions: the cross-dressed girl/boy disguise of Lord Summerisle – its ambiguity and innocent covering belies its power and malign intention – the punch-fool outfit, itself often disguising wily knowledge and malicious provocation, instead covers a serious but fundamentally innocent man.

Nevertheless, there is a deeply ingrained order in the islanders' culture, given historical weight through Summerisle's account of the society's development from his Grandfather's introduction of Paganism in 1868. This acute refraction of the contemporary western lifestyle has upset the standard utilisation of fundamental cultural parameters. First, in time, in the sense of regular occurrences of sacred-profane alterations that mark important periods of social life or even provide the measure of the passage of time itself – especially ritual celebrations and working routines.[15] Second, in space, in the sense of place where socially designated and culturally specific events are undergone; these reflect philosophical or cosmological conceptions. Most blatant in the film are the intentionally 'disturbing' settings for rituals and sacrifice – from the tethered beetle in the child's school-desk, to the fertility inducing activities amidst ancient stone circles, as well as the offerings in the graveyard. Krzywinska explains the historic relevance of one of these activities:

> The rite of leaping over fire, according to Frazer and corroborated by Hutton, is a tradition associated with Beltane (a term often used to describe the rites held on May Eve). As Frazer writes: 'In the central Highlands of Scotland bonfires, known as the Beltane fires, were formerly kindled with great ceremony on the first of May'. Celtic culture has been subject to the mythic imagination since at least the 18th century Celtic Revival. *The Wicker Man* draws on such rich sources, and they are framed by the context of Frazer's studies in which Scottish Beltane is seen as a rite in which the fertility of humans and animals was sustained by the

---

14 Schultz and Lavenda, *Cultural Anthropology,* p. 180.
15 See Leach, *Rethinking Anthropology.*

'blessing' of fire. The resonant coding of the chanting naked women jumping over the fire is further substantiated by the presence of the standing stones, evoking the mystique of the prehistoric past. As the standing stones are significant features in British cinema of the occult, they require closer consideration.[16]

Rituals and Sacrifice

Cosmologies collide in the film; we have the animistic islanders contrasted with the monotheistic Christian mainlander. We witness the colourful musical rituals in contrast to the solemn Christian practices; we spy on the reproductive fertility rites, the celebration of life and reincarnation, and we become engrossed, almost personally involved, in the final human sacrifice – lost in flames.

To the supposed scientific and would-be objective eye of the anthropologist, this is just another record of a dramatic cultural event. Many ethnographic films include scenes of violence against animals and people, often in gory detail: sometimes more shocking for the uninitiated than Howie's immolation. Of course, the audience's association with, and perhaps sympathy for, Howie is part of the emotional reaction to his ending. But surely there was good reason to sacrifice him in the minds of the islanders (let us not be ethnocentric). His death would ensure the next harvest and moreover, Howie's loss of life is only temporary, as he will be reincarnated. Any anthropologist could recount similar examples from other cultures: Frazer gives us examples in *The Golden Bough*, including that of ancient Thessaly, where kings were sacrificed to the Gods if harvests failed. Similarly, the Shilluk people of East Africa sacrifice their king if he becomes infirm, to ensure that his weakness is not transmitted to the crops.[17]

And is it not part of a uniformed serviceman's remit to anticipate a violent end? To sacrifice their life for the sake of their society and its continuing existence? It could be argued that Howie offered himself

---

[16] Krzywinska, *A Skin for Dancing In*, p. 84.
[17] Lienhardt, *Social Anthropology*, p. 148.

78

to, and was sacrificed by, the mainland community. Lienhardt, in a discussion of belief and knowledge, explores the reasons for sacrifice, which he sees as a universal human activity that remains in a variety of forms, often symbolic. He draws attention to the essential social aspect of this cultural activity:

> The sociological meaning of sacrifice has begun to be suggested when we have accepted it as a way of servicing the gods, and seen what those gods mean in relation to social life and human relations, how they correspond to the sharing of interests within different communities and sections of communities. From this point of view sacrifice to a common god is a sign and a strengthening of the common life.[18]

It would seem that Sergeant Howie's sacrifice occurred on at least two levels. He exemplified the cosmology of the islanders and brought them together in the most profound ritual of their cultural repertoire. On another level, he died for his own country; as a uniformed member his own personality and desires have been subsumed by the expectations of his culture's authorities. 'The Nation' mourns death in the line of duty through official state acknowledgement broadcast through the media. Sergeant Howie's death has import for the islanders and the mainlanders in that, paradoxically, it seems to strengthen their respective senses of community: in death his personality has been erased, but his cultural persona is elevated.

Clash of Cultures: An ongoing theme

With its clash of cultures, the head-on confrontation of ideologies, the violent meeting and spectacular result, *The Wicker Man* has peculiar resonance to contemporary geo-political events, where people from different cultural backgrounds are engaging in conflict, or becoming essentialised and demonised through immigration policies or as a result of acts of terrorism. Simplistic and politically driven portraits of different cultures and communities are common fare in today's

---

[18]   Lienhardt, *Social Anthropology,* p. 148.

media. The state's representatives of power, in the guise of soldiers and the police, regularly interact with foreign populations or people seen as 'other' than the mainland community. There is little room for thoughtful interpretation, less effort at understanding, and the option of tolerance is increasingly ignored: cultural relativity is rarely encountered.

Sergeant Howie, with his implacably ethnocentric outlook, his inflexibility and intolerance, his manifest willingness to employ coercive authority to achieve his goals, becomes the personification of the nation-state, the mainland, the United Kingdom (he transcends his Scottish location). And it is not only place that is superseded; time also becomes irrelevant. The film addresses the fundamental human cultural issue of power, and does so through a representation of group identity derived from a particular community, and the way this isolates the 'other'.

Just as most isolated communities are wary of the 'stranger', so the islanders are not forthcoming in answering questions about their neighbours and activities. Yet they readily surrender explanations about their culture when questioned; as happens in the best of ethnographic film, we learn about the reproductive and fertility symbols, the curative 'sympathetic' medicine, the purpose of fire-jumping. In essence what becomes apparent are the meanings of their cultural practices as well as their agrarian economy. Similarly, as a close face-to-face community they are ready to come together in times of adversity, and potentially sacrifice some of their own population for a greater communal goal – or better still, sacrifice an outsider. Again, we see reflections of the mainland community and its willingness to sacrifice its own people, in this case the uniformed services, and more easily recognisable representatives of another community, in order to achieve the larger society's goals.

The Wicker Man *as an Ethnographic Film*

Through Sergeant Howie's research, an explanation and record has been made of the islanders' 'Wicker Man' culture. Its rituals, and details of the economic, political, religious, family and even medical

characteristics are all there for interpretative use. We may consider this film as an archive, and tangible evidence of a cultural group. But we know the film is not 'true'. It is a fiction, a story – not a documentary. And yet, even if it fails us on the 'reality' test, it is on the extreme end of a continuum between fact and fiction in the ethnographic canon that embraces many set-ups, staged constructions, and re-enactments of cultural activities. It certainly satisfies the criteria that Heider sets out for a Naïve Ethnographic Film in that it has 'ethnographic import'.

However, in a profound way the film is more than Naïve Ethnographic Film; there is something genuine about it in its well-researched ritual details, costume and behaviour, at the very least. One of the film's strengths is its portrayal of our own 'mainland' culture *in extremis*. This can be observed in the personification of values that is Sergeant Howie and the refracted, distorted image of our culture that has become Lord Summerisle's island community. Furthermore, its deeper relevance is seen in the fundamental symbols, desires, rituals and fears relating to group cohesion, cosmology, reproduction and survival that form the bedrock of the film and speak to all human cultures and each of us as individuals.

In this film the creators have not recorded just one single 'disappearing world'. Rather, they have captured aspects of 'all our yesterdays'; it is a form of ethnographic film that has universal importance in that it challenges our understanding of both our own culture and those of others.

Bibliography

Anderson, R. and Connolly, B. (Directors), *First Contact* (Documentary Educational Resources, 1983).

Cheater, A., *Social Anthropology: An alternative introduction* (London: Routledge, 1989).

Flaherty, R. (Director), *Nanook of the North* (USA: MOMA and CONT/McG-H, 1922).

Frazer, J., *The Golden Bough* (Oxford: Oxford University Press, 1922).

_____, *The Golden Bough: A study in magic and religion. A new abridgement from the second and third editions*, ed. R. Fraser (Oxford: Oxford University Press, 1994).

Gardner, R. and Marshalls, J. (Directors), *The Hunters* (UK: Royal Anthropological Institute, 1956).

Hardy, R. (Director), *The Wicker Man – Special Edition Director's Cut* (Canal+, [1973] 2002).

Heider, K., *Ethnographic Film* (Austin: University of Texas Press, 1976).

Krzywinska, T., *A Skin for Dancing in: Possession, witchcraft and voodoo in film* (Wiltshire: Flicks Books, 2000).

Leach, E., *Rethinking Anthropology* (London: Athlone Press, 1961).

Levi-Strauss, C., *Structural Anthropology* (New York: Doubleday Anchor, 1967).

Lienhardt, G., *Social Anthropology* (Oxford: Oxford University Press, 1964).

Loizos, P., *Innovation in Ethnographic Film: From innocence to self-consciousness 1955-1985* (Manchester: Manchester University Press, 1993).

Nichols, B., *Ideology and the Image: Social representation in the cinema and other media* (Bloomington: Indiana University Press, 1981).

Ruby, J., 'Visual Anthropology', in *Encyclopedia of Cultural Anthropology*, ed. by D. Levinson and M. Ember (New York: Henry Holt and Company, 1996).

Schultz, E. and Lavenda, R., *Cultural Anthropology: A perspective on the human condition* (London: Mayfield Publishing Co., 1995).

Tylor, E., *Primitive Culture* (London: John Murray, 1871).

The Folklore Fallacy: A folkloristic/ filmic perspective on *The Wicker Man*

Mikel J. Koven

The Wicker Man is a film of particular interest to folklorists: here is a film which foregrounds and makes explicit the relationship between horror cinema, particularly horror cinema about Paganism and witchcraft, and its folkloric roots. The film's director, Robin Hardy, and its screenwriter, Anthony Shaffer, have made equally explicit their extensive research into Britain's Pagan past in order to realise their film. But *The Wicker Man* is furthermore a central film in discussing the relationship between folklore and popular culture, specifically popular film: for the kinds of research that Hardy and Shaffer have done raise several significant problems in the relationship between these two media. It is these points of convergence that this chapter discusses.

The folklore discourse within *The Wicker Man* coalesces around the film's reconstruction of an imaginary Celtic Pagan past which has been revived on a remote Scottish island by the fictional laird, Lord Summerisle (Christopher Lee). In this respect, the film attempts to revive diegetically an unselfconsciously Victorian perception of Celtic Paganism. Specifically, the film's titular, climactic set-piece, in which the central protagonist Sergeant Neil Howie (Edward Woodward) is burned alive in a sacrifice to the goddess Nuada to ensure the island's agrarian prosperity, is crucial here. It is based largely on the description of this rite in Sir James G. Frazer's *The Golden Bough*. But it is this interpretation of Frazer, of seeing *The Golden Bough* as an *historical* rather than a *folkloristic* description, which colours the entire film's folkloristic discourse – the film's 'folkloristic fallacy' as I have called it. This misinterpretation, in

many respects, results in a confusion regarding the different genres of oral folklore: Hardy and Shaffer do not seem to recognise that the 'Wicker Colossus' story, as it appears in Frazer and his own sources (namely, Julius Caesar's *Gallic Wars*), is a legend told about one culture *by a different culture*. In this respect, as legend, the story that the ancient Celts burned people alive as sacrifices in these wicker colossi needs to be seen, not as literally true, but as legendary. Elliott Oring has noted:

> Legends are considered narratives which focus on a single episode, an episode which is presented as miraculous, uncanny, bizarre, or sometimes embarrassing. The narration of a legend is, in a sense, the negotiation of the truth of these episodes. This is not to say that legends are always held to be true, as some scholars have claimed, but that at the core of the legend is an evaluation of its truth status. [. . .] This diversity of opinion does not negate the status of the narrative as legend because, whatever the opinion, the truth status of the narrative is what is being negotiated. In a legend, the question of truth must be *entertained* even if that truth is ultimately rejected. Thus, the legend often depicts the improbable with the world of the possible. The legend never asks for the suspension of disbelief. It is concerned with creating a narrative whose truth is at least worthy of deliberation; consequently, the art of legendry engages the listener's sense of the possible.[1]

To see the narrative of the wicker colossus of the ancient Celts, in particular their burning of human sacrifices within, as *legend* is to engage in a debate about whether or not people *really did* such a thing; but the debate is engaged in *by a culture other than the one portrayed in the episode*. That is, legends are, in addition to negotiations about the possible, negotiations about the Other. To see the 'wicker colossus' episode as legend, in part, is to see a negotiation of whether such 'barbarity' could have been perpetuated by non-Christians/non-Romans (depending upon the source of the legend), thereby creating a visceral distinction between 'us' (Frazer's Victorian Britons or Caesar's Republican Romans) and 'them' (the ancient pre-Christian Celts or cultures deserving to be conquered and

---

[1] Oring, 'Folk Narratives', p. 125; emphasis in original.

occupied); the legend genre demands such questions be discussed, even if ultimately discounted. And had the makers of *The Wicker Man* engaged in such debate, or presented the film's dénouement as a discursive episode, this current work would be rendered moot.

Unfortunately, in a series of interviews and documentaries surrounding *The Wicker Man*, both Hardy and Shaffer have made absolutely explicit the source materials which inspired the film: namely and primarily, *The Golden Bough*. More significantly, however, both men, well-read and erudite, appear to believe in the literal truth of Frazer's depiction. As Robin Hardy himself noted on the New Orleans television show, *Critic's Choice* in 1978, he wanted to recreate 'what a pagan society was like.'[2] This is a perspective that Hardy has maintained in the more than 30 years since the film was made. However, that Frazer's work is used uncritically by Hardy and Shaffer becomes highly problematic, in that they unintentionally reproduce many of the flaws of Frazer's original. This is not the place to go into tremendous detail about the problems in *The Golden Bough*, particularly for contemporary folklorists and anthropologists, but some context is required.

The word 'Folk-Lore', coined by the antiquarian collector William John Thoms in a letter published in the *Athenaeum* on 22 August 1846, as a replacement for the then-used term 'popular antiquities', emerged concurrent with the scientific discourse of anthropology in the middle of the century. This brought folklore from a hobby of the amateur collector to an academic discourse, largely through two works by the so-called 'father of anthropology', E. B. Tylor:[3] *Researches into the Early History of Mankind* (1865) and *Primitive Culture* (1871). In the former, as Richard Dorson summarises:

Folklore represented the contemporary superstitions and nursery tales of civilized peoples. Mythology preserved the explanation in story form which all peoples, from the primitive to the highly developed, fashioned to account for their supernatural origins. Folklore belonged only to the last and highest stage of cultural

---

[2] Hardy, quoted from *Critic's Choice with Stirling Smith*.
[3] Dorson, *The British Folklorists*, p. 187.

progression and *embodied survivals from the earlier stages*. Mythology appeared at all stages, but in varying degrees of simplicity and sophistication according to the advancement of the race.[4]

Tylor took the then popular theories of biological evolution, and applied them to cultural development, where cultures gradually *evolved* from states of primitive savagery to the highest levels of civilisation. He developed this idea of cultural survivals further in his *Primitive Culture*, wherein he identified still existent practices of superstition and forms of animism which had survived from the primitive past of a culture:

> While the main march of mankind is upward, from savagery through barbarism to ascending levels of civilization, relics of savagery, such as witchcraft, still survive among civilized peoples, and occasionally burst into revivals, as in the fad of spiritualism, a revival of primitive sorcery.[5]

It is this theory of survivals which directly informed Cambridge don James Frazer in 1890 to publish, firstly in two volumes, *The Golden Bough*, which traces the cultural development from animistic primitivism through to civilised religious practices as a massive, global, and significantly generalised study in religious survivals. Frazer was not immune to attacks by other scholars, including a number of folklorists who in 1878 formed The Folk-Lore Society (which has survived till the present). For example, Andrew Lang, while more or less supporting the Tylorian theory of survivals, attacked Frazer's scholarship, which he saw as 'based on conjecture, false analogy, unwarranted surmise, and invalid reference.'[6] More pertinently, George Laurence Gomme criticised Frazer for his 'free linkage of customs and rites from unlike cultures',[7] and this is one of the major problems of Frazer for contemporary folklorists and anthropologists. And, by their uncritical reading of Frazer, these criticisms carry over into Hardy and Shaffer's *The Wicker Man*, as I discuss

[handwritten in left margin: Contemporary criticisms of Frazer]

---

[4] Dorson, *The British Folklorists*, p. 187; emphasis added.
[5] Dorson, *The British Folklorists*, p. 193.
[6] Dorson, *The British Folklorists*, p. 285.
[7] Dorson, *The British Folklorists*, p. 284.

below. Perhaps significantly, what the director and screenwriter demonstrate by their unquestioning acceptance of *The Golden Bough*'s 'truths', is Frazer's popularity beyond the scholarly arena. As Dorson notes, 'a reading public indifferent to scholarly polemics relished the 'golden treasury of stories for grown-up children' and appreciated learning about *the less advanced peoples within the Empire*.'[8] Hardy and Shaffer are just such a latter-day reading public for *The Golden Bough*, and their 'indifference' towards the academic dimension of the work manifests itself in the film.

Just as popular film is of peripheral interest for the majority of contemporary folklorists, so too is anthropological verisimilitude of secondary importance to horror film makers. Instead of recreating a modern survival of Britain's Pagan past, Hardy and Shaffer (working clearly within the context of Frazer's popular reading audience) instead reproduce a late Victorian reconstruction of what such a past might have been like, complete with the ideology of the Empire. Perhaps parenthetically, it *could* be argued that the diegetic society Hardy and Shaffer create is intentionally a Victorian reconstruction, rather than any attempt at an authentic and historically accurate depiction of Britain's Pagan past: we are told that the first Lord Summerisle re-established the 'old gods' in 1868, and so not only *might* he have been familiar with Tylor's *Early History of Mankind*, but he certainly would have been aware of the discussion of cultural survivals which was part of the intellectual *zeitgeist*.[9] So in some respects, the Paganism practised on Summerisle can be seen to be a direct result of this (fictional) mid-Victorian revival. However, Robin Hardy himself undermines such a theory in interviews wherein he asserts the accuracy of this depiction of Celtic Paganism, rather than the accuracy of it as Victorian reconstruction.[10]

---

[8] Dorson, *The British Folklorists*, p. 287; emphasis added.

[9] Hardy and Shaffer, *The Wicker Man*, p. 132.

[10] For example see the commentary track on the 2001 Warner Home Video DVD release of the director's cut of *The Wicker Man*, as well as David Gregory's 2001 documentary *The Wicker Man Enigma*, also on the same DVD set. Also see Abbott and Leven's 2001 documentary, *Burnt Offering: The Cult of the Wicker Man*, originally broadcast on Channel 4 in the UK.

Hardy and Shaffer dipped liberally into *The Golden Bough* in order to create their world of Summerisle, but this 'dipping' was highly selective: Frazer's 62nd chapter on 'The Fire-Festivals of Europe', wherein he notes the pan-European (if not universal) significance of certain bonfire rites, and his lengthy discussion of the Scottish Beltane festival (celebrated on the first of May), make up much of the context for *The Wicker Man*'s diegesis. Frazer himself included a chapter-length survey outlining the variety of interpretive contexts, largely anthropological in scope, for discussing such fire festivals, although Hardy and Shaffer seem not to have recognised the diversity of interpretive perspectives which the chapter depicts. At least in this chapter, Frazer avoided the superficial trap of bestowing a single interpretation on the fire festivals of Europe, but demonstrated a contemporary weighing up of Mannhardt's so-called Solar Theory, which argues that the lighting of enormous bonfires is a kind of mimicking of the sun's regenerative powers.[11] This is contrasted with Purification Theory, which sees these bonfires as a means of purifying the land of harmful influences or evil spirits.[12] Frazer tended to agree with this latter interpretation, noting that it 'appears more probable and more in accordance with the evidence than the opposing theory of their connexion [sic] with the sun.' It is significant, moreover, that Frazer rationalised his acceptance of this theory on the grounds that it was ethnographically verified: 'it is to be observed that the people who practise the fire-customs appear never to allege the solar theory in explanation of them, while on the contrary they do frequently and emphatically put forward the purificatory theory.'[13] While throughout much of *The Golden Bough*, Frazer tended toward a symbolic interpretation along Mannhardtian lines, on the meaning of fire festivals at least, he opted for the simpler explanation of purification ritual.[14] In many

---

[11]   Frazer, *The Golden Bough*, pp. 745-50.

[12]   Frazer, *The Golden Bough,* pp. 750-53.

[13]   Frazer, *The Golden Bough,* p.753, p. 751.

[14]   Alfred Nutt, another contemporary of Frazer's, praised *The Golden Bough* specifically for the author's use of Mannhardt. Nutt wrote, 'their names will remain indissolubly linked together in the history of folklore scholarship.'

respects, *The Wicker Man* owes more to the solar theories of Wilhelm Mannhardt than to James G. Frazer, but it is through Frazer that Hardy and Shaffer received their information.

The relationship between *The Golden Bough* and *The Wicker Man*, however, is absolutely explicit in the depiction of the film's titular construction. In Frazer's 64th chapter, 'The Burning of Human Beings in the Fires', the author noted that the fire festivals were survivals of Pagan-past rites of human sacrifice, specifically the Scottish Beltane festival. This section of Frazer is significant enough to quote at length:

> Of human sacrifices offered on these occasions the most unequivocal traces, as we have seen, are those which, about a hundred years ago, still lingered at the Beltane fires in the Highlands of Scotland, that is, among a Celtic people who, situated in a remote corner of Europe and almost completely isolated from foreign influence, had till then conserved their old heathenism better perhaps than any other people in the West of Europe. It is significant, therefore, that human sacrifices by fire are known, on unquestionable evidence, to have been systematically practised by the Celts. The earliest description of these sacrifices has been bequeathed to us by Julius Caesar.[15]

What Nutt appreciated was the linking of custom with storytelling, song and riddle, from the evolutionary/survival perspective, rather than the so-called 'diffusionist' position, which stated that narrative, song, riddle, etc. disseminated out and travelled largely independently from custom and ritual (Dorson, *The British Folklorists*, p. 284).

[15] In Caesar's account, the general noted: 'the nation of all the Gauls is extremely devoted to superstitious rites; and on that account they who are troubled with unusually severe diseases, and they who are engaged in battles and dangers, either sacrifice men as victims, or vow that they will sacrifice them, and employ the Druids as the performers of those sacrifices; because they think that unless the life of a man be offered for the life of a man, the mind of the immortal gods can not be rendered propitious, and they have sacrifices of that kind ordained for national purposes. Others have figures of vast size, the limbs of which formed of osiers they fill with living men, which being set on fire, the men perish enveloped in the flames. They consider that the oblation of such as have been taken in theft, or in robbery, or any other offence, is more acceptable to the immortal gods; but when a supply of that class is wanting, they have recourse to the oblation of even the innocent' (Caesar, VI,16).

As conqueror of the hitherto independent Celts of Gaul, Caesar had ample opportunity of observing the national Celtic religion and manners, while these were still fresh and crisp from the native mind and had not yet been fused in the melting-pot of Roman civilisation. With his own notes Caesar appears to have incorporated the observations of a Greek explorer, by name Posidonius, who travelled in Gaul about fifty years before Caesar carried the Roman arms to the English Channel. The Greek geographer Strabo and the historian Diodorus seem also to have derived their descriptions of the Celtic sacrifices from the work of Posidonius, but independently of each other, and of Caesar, for each of the three derivative accounts contain some details which are not to be found in either of the others. By combining them, therefore, we can restore the original account of Posidonius with some probability, and thus obtain a picture of the sacrifices offered by the Celts of Gaul at the close of the second century before our era. The following seem to have been the main outlines of the custom. Condemned criminals were reserved by the Celts in order to be sacrificed to the gods at a great festival which took place once in every five years. The more there were of such victims, the greater was believed to be the fertility of the land. If there were not enough criminals to furnish victims, captives taken in war were immolated to supply the deficiency. When the time came the victims were sacrificed by the Druids or priests. Some they shot down with arrows, some they impaled, and some they burned alive in the following manner. Colossal images of wicker-work or of wood and grass were constructed; these were filled with live men, cattle, and animals of other kinds; fire was then applied to the images, and they were burned with their living contents.[16]

In setting *The Wicker Man* on a remote Scottish island, Hardy and Shaffer were clearly informed by Frazer's assertion that the 'old heathenism' was, until recently, still in evidence in the remotest parts of the country. Where Hardy and Shaffer diverge from Frazer's account is in the nature of the sacrifice. *The Golden Bough* makes

---

[16]   Frazer, *The Golden Bough*, pp. 757-58.

explicit that those sacrificed were criminals or prisoners of war, not innocents like Howie, an aspect also noted by Caesar.[17]

As I noted above, contrary to Mannhardt's solar theory of ritual, the killing and burning of criminals and captured enemies was, for Frazer, more likely a purification ritual. Although Frazer was more inclined towards a Mannhardt-inspired interpretation of this ritual in an early edition of *The Golden Bough*, he revised his opinion in later editions. As Frazer noted:

> The Druidical sacrifices which we are considering were explained in a different way by W. Mannhardt. He supposed that the men whom the Druids burned in wicker-work images represented the spirits of vegetation, and accordingly that the custom of burning them was a magical ceremony intended to secure the necessary sunshine for the crops. Similarly, he seems to have inclined to the view that the animals which used to be burnt in the bonfires represented the cornspirit, which, as we saw in an earlier part of this work, is often supposed to assume the shape of an animal. This theory is no doubt tenable, and the great authority of W. Mannhardt entitles it to careful consideration. I adopted it in former editions of this book; but on reconsideration it seems to me on the whole to be less probable than the theory that the men and animals burnt in the fires perished in the character of witches. This latter view is strongly supported by the testimony of the people who celebrate the fire-festivals, since a popular name for the custom of kindling the fires is 'burning the witches,' effigies of witches are sometimes consumed in the flames, and the fires, their embers, or their ashes are supposed to furnish protection against witchcraft. On the other hand there is little to show that the effigies or the animals burnt in the fires are regarded by the people as representatives of the vegetation-spirit, and that the bonfires are sun-charms.[18]

Therefore, as Frazer himself observed, despite an earlier predilection towards solar theories to explain the rites of the ancient Celts, a

---

[17] Caesar, *The Gallic Wars*, VI,16, although Caesar does note that 'when a supply of that class [criminals] is [found] wanting, they have recourse to the oblation of even the innocent.'

[18] Frazer, *The Golden Bough*, pp. 762-63.

more considered argument was towards a purificatory interpretation of the rite. Again, as Frazer noted:

> If we are right in interpreting the modern European fire-festivals as attempts to break the power of witchcraft by burning or banning the witches and warlocks, it seems to follow that we must explain the human sacrifices of the Celts in the same manner; that is, we must suppose that the men whom the Druids burnt in wicker-work images were condemned to death on the ground that they were witches or wizards, and that the mode of execution by fire was chosen because burning alive is deemed the surest mode of getting rid of these noxious and dangerous beings.[19]

If we see the residents of Summerisle as burning the innocent Howie in order to appease Nuada (the ancient Celtic sun goddess) and bring prosperity back to the island's apple crop, we are working from a Mannhardtian solar theory perspective. What becomes clear, however, in looking at Hardy and Shaffer's source materials in the creation of *The Wicker Man*, is a demonstration of the absolute literal-mindedness of the diegesis's creators. They read Frazer, and an early edition of Frazer at that, and interpreted his depictions to be accurate, not discursive, as later editions of *The Golden Bough* retrospectively acknowledged. For the filmmakers, their intended project, using Frazer, was to recreate – accurately – Celtic rites. In so doing they missed Frazer's own, albeit belated, admission that such a depiction was being filtered through a very specific theoretical schema, namely, Mannhardt's solar theory.

This literal realisation of Frazer occurs throughout the film: as another example, at one point during his discussion of the burning of wicker-work effigies, Frazer noted that a false victim was sometimes chosen and much play was made of that person being about to be thrown into the flames. As Frazer also noted, 'the *pretend* victim was seized and a show made of throwing him into the flames, and for some time afterwards people affected to speak of him as dead.'[20] The

---

[19] Frazer, *The Golden Bough,* p. 761.

[20] Frazer, *The Golden Bough,* p. 756; emphasis added.

entire sense of play in *The Wicker Man*'s narrative can be seen as a dramatisation of this rite. Lord Summerisle's deception of Howie, specifically his use of Rowan as bait to get the gormless lawman to the island, creates Rowan as such a false victim. While at first, Howie can find no reference to Rowan ever having been alive, it quickly becomes apparent, to Howie at least, that she is dead. (The audience is equally denied any contrary information, so at this stage in the narrative development, we too believe Rowan is dead). That Rowan's death has been a ruse to trap the innocent Howie only becomes apparent at the film's dénouement. Hardy and Shaffer also throw in a miscellany of 'olde' motifs, some from Frazer, some from elsewhere, to realise their film. For example, Howie is put to sleep with the 'Hand of Glory', a dead woman's hand burned as a candle which induces a deep sleep: this also appears in Frazer's discussion of homeopathic magic.[21] This magical belief is not linked to the Beltane festival, nor Pagan human sacrifice rites, but it is there in the filmic mix. Frazer also discusses the use of virgins, like Howie, in human sacrifice, although these rites are explicitly (and significantly) non-European.[22] Elsewhere in the film we can see other forms of contagious and imitative magic rites being performed, like the small frog May Morrison puts into Myrtle's mouth to transfer her daughter's sore throat to the amphibian; or the animistic costumes worn in the May Day procession, including the Hobby Horse. These 'bits' of action and *mise-en-scene* are intended to evoke a feeling of authenticity within the diegesis, but instead, because of their original disparate temporal and spatial contexts, the effect is one of a folkloric amusement park.

Allan Brown noted that in the creation of Sergeant Howie, 'Shaffer and Hardy's perfect sacrifice would be a checklist, would contain *all* the attributes which had made one a perfect sacrifice. Shaffer and Hardy's victim would be a willing, king-like virgin fool.'[23] From a folkloric perspective, the problem here, and elsewhere within

---

[21] Frazer, *The Golden Bough*, p. 35.

[22] Frazer, *The Golden Bough*, pp. 164-65.

[23] Brown, *Inside 'The Wicker Man'*, p. 23.

the film, is that the idea of a 'checklist' of attributes is a literary contrivance and unlikely to be found in practice, beyond the fact that, as I noted above, the victims in the wicker colossus would probably have been criminals and/or witches, and their burning would have purged evil influences from the society.[24] This demonstrates, quite explicitly, that often when popular culture forms *do* folklore, they use all of it, every bit they can get their hands on, regardless of original context. The result is often a representational quagmire which does little to explore the people being represented. Instead, it unproblematically reproduces the ideology of the film's creators.

Hardy and Shaffer's folkloristic fallacy, however, goes deeper still: the filmmakers are solely dependent upon (and uncritical of) a single source for their material. Perhaps it is a bit too grand to expect verisimilitude of anthropological discourse in a low-budget horror/fantasy film; but what emerges from *The Wicker Man* is also a demonstration of the academic problems within Frazer. In discussing the meaning inherent within the fire festivals across Europe, Frazer notes that 'we can hardly help being struck by the resemblance which the [European fire festival] ceremonies bear to each other, at whatever time of the year and in whatever part of Europe they are celebrated.'[25] Victorian anthropology and folklore studies tended to conceive the world in grand master narratives. Based on surface comparisons, world cultures were seen to celebrate more-or-less the same calendrical and life-cycle ceremonies; any differences were seen as unimportant cultural deviances. These ideas were later popularised by Joseph Campbell, after the Second World War, as the mono-myth – his *Hero with a Thousand Faces* – that all cultures shared the same myths, just in different guises.

This approach, while superficially appearing to be egalitarian, is in actuality purely colonial: only from a point of cultural hegemony can one hold one's culture up as a template for other cultures and say that they are more or less the same. The later, more ethnographic

---

[24] Frazer, *The Golden Bough*, p. 757; but see papers by Sermon and James elsewhere in this volume for other perspectives on the veracity of this account.

[25] Frazer, *The Golden Bough*, p. 743.

studies, beginning with Malinowski for British anthropology and Boas for American anthropology, particularly after the Second World War, tended to embrace an insider oriented, experiential dimension to cultural practices. In other words, what Hardy and Shaffer attempted to do in *The Wicker Man* was to unproblematically literalise a colonialist agenda which sees the Celtic nations as an undifferentiated whole, and does not distinguish between the other cultural influences which may have affected Frazer's descriptions of the Beltane and sacrificial rites. And this is without questioning Frazer's unproblematic acceptance of the Classical source material he cites freely – specifically Caesar, who had his own agenda in seeing the Celts demonised as human-sacrificing savages. This depiction of the 'savage Celts' was further disseminated by Aylett Sammes, whose famous 1676 illustration of Caesar's 'wicker man' colossus was given by Hardy to *The Wicker Man*'s art director, Seamus Flannery to follow in the creation of the film's own wicker colossus. So in many respects, what we see in the film is a complex trajectory of influences: Caesar, working from reports by Posidonius and others, depicts the idea of the 'wicker man' as a Celtic sacrificial rite; this becomes graphically depicted in a seventeenth century version of *Gallic Wars*; the idea is again picked up by Frazer, who attempts to understand its meaning; his discussions find their way to Robin Hardy and Anthony Shaffer, who create their screenplay and realise the Frazerian world in the guise of Summerisle. This is further complicated by having Flannery base the art direction on Sammes' illustration. But then the bizarre really takes off: *The Wicker Man*, as a cult film, in turn influences at least two generations of modern Pagans, who, in attending the annual Wickerman Festival in Scotland and Burning Man Festival in Nevada, attempt to recreate the Celtic culture of Summerisle. Although these participants recognise that *The Wicker Man* is a fictional film, they do not necessarily question Hardy and Shaffer's source materials, particularly Frazer.[26] But, in

---

[26] It does, however, need to be noted that not all modern Pagans are under the impression that either *The Wicker Man* or *The Golden Bough* are either ethnographic or accurate in their depictions of Celtic rites or witchcraft. And neither do all modern Pagans attend these festivals.

their living recreation of Summerisle, they have, in fact, made Summerisle and its (neo-)/(pseudo-) Celtic rites real, in what, in legend-studies, is known as pseudo-ostension.[27]

While Robin Hardy, Anthony Shaffer and any other number of people associated with *The Wicker Man* may feel that the film is rooted within some kind of 'authentic folklore' because of the film-makers' use of Sir James G. Frazer's *The Golden Bough*, and that its literal realisation within the film is, in effect, an accurate realisation of ancient Celtic rites, they are working under what I have termed the 'folklore fallacy'. Notwithstanding any flaws within Frazer's approach, ideological issues inherent within Victorian anthropology and folklore studies, or other methodological problems, it is the indiscriminate inclusion of any and all forms of 'folklore' into the film's diegetic mix which creates this fallacy. Perhaps unintentionally, however, the film does operate within a significant folkloristic nexus: if we see *The Wicker Man* as but one text in a long line of cultural representations regarding Celtic/Druidic rites, from Caesar through Sammes and then Frazer to Hardy and Shaffer, and divorce the discourse from any consideration of 'authenticity', we can identify the distinct thread of the legend of the 'Wicker Man'.

Bibliography

Abbot, A. and Leven, R. (Directors), *Burnt Offering: The cult of 'The Wicker Man'* (Nobles Gate Ltd., 2001).

Brown, A., *Inside 'The Wicker Man': The morbid ingenuities* (London: Sidgwick and Jackson, 2000).

Caesar, J., *Gallic Wars*, trans. W. A. McDevitte and W. S. Bohn, *The Internet Classics Archive* http://classics.mit.edu/Caesar/gallic.html [Accessed 13 August 2004].

Campbell, J., *The Hero with a Thousand Faces* (London: Fontana Press, 1948, 1988).

---

[27] Koven, 'Candyman Can: Film and Ostension'.

Dorson, R. M., *The British Folklorists: A history* (Chicago: University of Chicago Press, 1968).

Frazer, J. G., *The Golden Bough* (New York: Macmillan, 1922, 1963).

Gregory, D., *The Wicker Man Enigma* (2002). Extra feature contained on DVD of *The Wicker Man – Special Edition Director's Cut*. dir. R. Hardy. Canal+. ([1973] 2002).

Hardy, R. (Director), *The Wicker Man – Special Edition Director's Cut* (Canal+, [1973] 2002).

Hardy, R. and A. Shaffer, *The Wicker Man* (London: Pan Books, 1978, 2000).

Koven, M. J., 'Candyman Can: Film and Ostension', *Contemporary Legend*, New Series 2 (1999), pp. 137-154.

Oring, E., 'Folk Narratives' *Folk Groups and Folklore Genres: An Introduction*, ed. Elliott Oring (Logan: Utah State University Press, 1986), pp. 121-46.

Smith, S., *Critics Choice with Stirling Smith* (1978). Extra feature contained on DVD of *The Wicker Man – Special Edition Director's Cut*. dir. R. Hardy. Canal+. ([1973] 2002).

Tylor, E. B., *Primitive Culture: Researches into the development of mythology, philosophy, religion, language, art, and custom*, 2nd ed (London: J. Murray, 1873).

_____, *Researches into the Early History of Mankind and the Development of Civilization*, 3rd ed (London: J. Murray, 1878).

The Wicker Man – Cult Film or Anti-Cult Film? Parallels and paradoxes in the representation of Paganism, Christianity and the law

Anthony J. Harper

AMONG THE INTRIGUING aspects of the film *The Wicker Man* are its reception and ensuing reputation. One can detect an apparent paradox between the way the film, over the years since 1973, has stayed in public consciousness as a kind of 'cult film', and the negative presentation of the island community of Summerisle as a 'cult'. The central contrast between Paganism and Christianity is associated with this paradox. Paganism is the intriguing and – for many people in 1973 – still somewhat unusual aspect of the film and it is contrasted with the supposed norm of the time (known to, if not accepted by, all), namely, Christianity.

This chapter will examine the paradoxical contrast between two differing attitudes, religions or philosophies by means of an analysis of two statements made in the film. They both occur, probably not by coincidence, in Scene 10 of both the theatrical version and the director's cut of the film, entitled 'Lord Summerisle'. In that scene the film's two protagonists are in debate. Lord Summerisle, the feudal laird of the island, confronted with the accusation that a murder has taken place, demurs at the possibility, claiming 'we're a very religious people.' Then Howie, the police sergeant investigating the apparent disappearance of a child, attacks the practices that he finds current on the island, telling Lord Summerisle that this is 'a Christian country.'

Neither of these two protagonists is a particularly sympathetic

figure with whom the audience can readily empathise or might wish to empathise. Indeed, both seem on occasions decidedly unattractive. Each plays off the other, and they have, for example, been described as 'one another's 'other'.'[1] This lack of a hero with whom one may unequivocally identify can be viewed as a positive aspect of the film, since the audience is therefore able to examine all statements from the two figures without the danger of a simple, because exclusive, acceptance of a single set of sentiments on the basis of identification with the relevant character concerned. Howie's and Summerisle's respective statements may therefore be viewed as having a Brechtian *Verfremdungseffekt* (alienation or distancing effect), intended to disturb us, to distance us from the action and make us reflect on the words or even respond by reacting against them.

The growth of interest in, or even personal existential identification with, Pagan traditions might be attributed to various strands of twentieth century culture. Sir James Frazer's famous study *The Golden Bough* first appeared in 1890 and soon stimulated great cultural interest far beyond its own specialised sphere; we shall return to this work in a moment. Margaret Murray's *The Witch Cult in Western Europe*, a sensational and controversial work, now largely rejected, appeared in 1921; the works of Gerald Gardner, whose first novel *A Goddess Arrives* appeared in 1941, are usually regarded as having founded the development known as Wicca. These were followed by a number of further works such as *Witchcraft Today*.[2] This trend was ultimately legitimised when the last Witchcraft Act was repealed in Britain in 1951; finally, there was the hippie culture developing in the 1960s, which was the forerunner of what later came to be called New Age thinking. Although New Age ideas are by no means identical with specific Pagan practice, all these developments were friendly, or at least open, towards Paganism and meant that for some people Paganism was not an

---

[1] Brass, 'Reel Images of the Land (Beyond the Forest)', p. 28.

[2] Murray, *The Witch Cult in Western Europe*, followed by *The Divine King in England*; Gardner, *A Goddess Arrives* and Gardner and Murray, *Witchcraft Today*.

unknown factor in British culture by 1973. Nevertheless, for the majority of filmgoers the depiction of a full-blown Pagan cult or religion being followed somewhere in contemporary Britain (even if only on its most extreme north western periphery, a location perhaps stereotypically associated with eccentric cultures) was an unusual, even shocking, aspect of the film in 1973. To some extent, the film can be seen as foreshadowing a further growth of interest in Paganism and in the movements that have been developing since that time, and which are often summed up in the term 'Neo-Paganism'.

Although Lord Summerisle's assertion of the islanders' religiosity might appear excessive at first hearing, there is some justification for the view that the cult being practised on the island is in fact a religion, in that it completely informs the lives of the inhabitants and creates or nurtures their spirituality. In any case, the word 'cult' has often been used in a derogatory sense as a substitute description for a 'religion'. Summerisle's claim represents a potential line of defence, so that the killing at the end of the film can be viewed as sacrifice and not murder.

Much of the representation of Paganism appears to be based on Frazer's *The Golden Bough*. In 1890 its original subtitle in the preliminary version was 'A Study in Comparative Religion', but this was altered in the later full-length versions, from 1900 onwards, to 'A Study in Magic and Religion'. There is now general agreement that Frazer's findings are often questionable at the very least, if not inaccurate, but that does not alter the massive cultural impact of his work.[3] Many features of the religion of Pagan prehistory, and folkloristic survivals of the same, are introduced into the film. In many cases these stem from Frazer's research.[4]

A list of such pagan motifs can very easily be drawn up, but is unlikely to be exhaustive. Thus there is, for example, the theme of the hare, a symbol of immortality, the motif of the Green Man (the name of the pub on the island, but not very much exploited in the

---

[3]   Cf. Temple in his introduction to Frazer, *The Illustrated Golden Bough*, pp. 6-7.

[4]   See Koven's paper in this volume.

film), the phallic symbol of the maypole, the dance and fire ceremony, the ceremony with masks, and so on. Reference to these and many other motifs can be accessed easily in the index of Frazer's work.[5]

Central to many of these phenomena is the relationship between humanity and nature and the question of fertility, of plants, animals and human beings. It is a good guess that these featured in prehistoric Paganism as well as in later historical times that are more directly available to researchers. But there are also motifs from other periods. Going right back to the Neolithic, there is the stone circle, conveniently situated right by the castle on a nice level patch of ground; the circle has trilithons so that we do not miss the reference to Stonehenge, the only circle in the British Isles possessing that feature. Probably more important here than archaeological accuracy is the association of Stonehenge, in the popular mind, with presumed pre-Christian rites such as the celebration of the midsummer sunrise. A sun god, a sea god, and a goddess of the harvest are mentioned at different points in the film.

The wicker man motif itself is based on stories by classical writers such as Diodorus Siculus ('*kollosson*'), Strabo and Julius Caesar ('*immanu magnitudine simulacra*') that may or may not be based on fact about the Druids (who are otherwise not mentioned).[6] There is the motif of the skull and crossbones, associated with Scottish Freemasonry from the seventeenth century onwards, and of course still to be seen in many Scottish cemeteries. There is mention of a life force that seems to reflect the vitalism of the turn of the century around 1900. The phenomenal fertility of the island, at least until immediately prior to the film's action, an area washed by the gulf stream, appears to be a possible reference to the fertile land settled by the Findhorn community. The Findhorn community was, and is, an alternative life-style commune that grew up in the North of Scotland in the post-war period not long before the time-

---

[5]   Cf. Krzywinska, *A Skin for Dancing In,* pp. 85-86.

[6]   Diodorus Siculus, *Histories,* XXXI, pp. 2-5; Strabo, *Geographia,* Book IV; Julius Caesar, *Gallic Wars,* Book VI, Ch. XVI; all cited in Piggott, *The Druids,* p. 99.

setting of the film. Although the eclectic amalgam of these and other similar motifs would certainly not stand up to academic scrutiny as a study of any particular religion in any particular period, the use of Frazer seems intelligent and, probably for all except academic specialists, is blended successfully with a number of other motifs. As was the case with Jessie L. Weston's now outmoded study *From Ritual to Romance* – the major source for T. S. Eliot's famous poem 'The Waste Land'[7] (itself not by any means dissimilar in theme from that of our film) – works such as *The Golden Bough* have a symbolic influence out of all proportion to their eventual academic value.

If the amalgam in the film is artistically successful then part of that achievement can be attributed to the fact that the presentation of Paganism accords with the vaguely New Age music in the background (the term 'New Age' is of course anachronistic for the year 1973). The pagan themes combine well with the folk music style of 'Corn Rigs and Barley Rigs' and the other songs (even though much of the repertoire of the film is not authentic folk song). This is in part due to the identification of the folk revival, which had got well under way in the late 1960s, with an alternative, anti-establishment culture.

In other regards *The Wicker Man* conforms to accepted historical accounts. It rightly avoids asserting that Paganism, or similar religions, had existed continuously from prehistoric or even early historic times; modern researchers have made themselves very clear on this historical point.[8] Within the film Lord Summerisle is unambiguous on the same point, explaining that the cult or religion was introduced by his grandfather in the nineteenth century and was perceived and accepted as bringing prosperity and fertility to the island.

Initially this religion seems to have some attractive features, such as an apparently joyful and affirmative attitude towards life,

---

[7] Eliot, 'The Waste Land', pp. 61-86.

[8] Cf. Hutton, *The Pagan Religions of the Ancient British Isles,* pp. 43-79 and pp. 340-41; also de Blécourt, *Witchcraft and Magic in Europe*, pp. 205-19.

together with a relaxed attitude towards sexuality. Although the pub song about the landlord's daughter is an unimpressive statement of the latter, the scene of the mating snails in the director's cut is more successful. But we swiftly realise that this nature religion is one in which the islanders both love and fear nature, and from quite early on in the film the failure of the harvest represents a sinister or at least unsettling undertone. This leads on with increasing inevitability to the horrific human sacrifice at the conclusion of *The Wicker Man*, which enables one justifiably to call it a horror film, even though it eschews the genre's conventional iconographic repertoire of haunted houses and sensational effects. Rather than the conclusion being a deliberately and generically excessive moment of *grand guignol*, the Summerislanders' belief system is a religion that demands sacrifice of a sort contravening civilised norms. As such, Howie's immolation occurs well within the bounds of the narrative's internal logic.

We do not know how far back in prehistoric antiquity such rites may have been practised. It is arguable that human sacrifice was not a regular ritual or normal practice in the Neolithic and earlier periods, but rather a feature stemming from the late Bronze and Iron Ages when the climate was deteriorating, the population increasing, and authoritarian and patriarchal structures developing, creating pressures such as aggression and fear in the population. A recent collection of essays on prehistoric ceremony edited by Alex Gibson and Derek Simpson and titled *Prehistoric Ritual and Religion* contains only one reference to sacrifice, human or animal.[9] Most modern Pagans, too, would dissent strongly from the idea that human sacrifice is an inevitable or necessary part of their rituals.

In any case, there still seems to be much controversy about the historical reliability of the wicker man motif.[10] To quote just two commentators: Peter Beresford Ellis sees a paucity of evidence for human sacrifice and points to contemporary classical propaganda against the Celts and Druids.[11] For Stuart Piggott, on the other

---

[9]   Gibson and Simpson, *Prehistoric Ritual and Religion,* p. 200.
[10]   See Sermon's paper in this volume.
[11]   Ellis, *The Druids,* pp. 144-52; Piggott, *The Druids,* p. 99.

hand, 'it is hardly realistic to exculpate the Druids for participating, probably actively, in both the beliefs and practice involved in human sacrifice.'[12] At any rate, Lord Summerisle's claim that the islanders are a very religious people is perfectly tenable within the context of the film, but at the same time, and more importantly, it raises the question about the quality and values of this religion; ultimately its Pagan practices are shown in a sinister light and culminate in the horrific finale. It is a religion, but is it one that a civilised society can possibly consider adopting?

The other statement in Scene 10 was that by Howie, the police sergeant, who stated that this is 'a Christian country.' It is difficult to assess nowadays how far those words can be considered accurate for the year 1973. It is additionally difficult to discern whether the country is to be considered as Great Britain, or as Scotland alone. For Scotland, or for the Highland areas of Scotland at any rate, it was possibly still tenable at that time, but at the least the assertion raises an initial question mark in the mind of the modern viewer. There is not very much about Christianity in the earlier part of the original theatrical version of the film and in any case what we do hear and see is associated with just one person, Howie, to a much greater extent than Paganism is associated with Lord Summerisle alone. Just as many Pagans would demur at the idea of human sacrifice, so too many Christians would demur at seeing Howie as the typical or stereotypical Christian.

The director's cut begins with an extensive scene entitled 'Mainland' (Scene 1, missing in the theatrical version) which shows us, for the only sustained period in the film, the mainland 'normality', as one might say. This longer version offers much more about Howie than we see in the theatrical version and in doing so strengthens his association with Christianity, although some parts of the 'Mainland' scene are incorporated in the original cut.[13] The precise denomination of Howie's Christianity is left somewhat vague, just as Summerisle is marked by an amalgam of paganism. The scene indicates

---

[12] Piggott, *The Druids,* p. 99.

[13] See Jones, 'Now a Major Motion Picture?'

Protestantism, with Howie taking the communion cup (this was not possible for the laity in a Roman Catholic church in 1973), in a church with stained glass windows, presumably therefore the Scottish Episcopal Church (the equivalent of the Church of England in Scotland), which is strong in parts of the Highlands. (It is not absolutely impossible, however, that a Church of Scotland church might have some stained glass windows). For the Western Highlands (as indicated by the strong Gaelic lilt) one might have expected the presence of either the Free Church of Scotland, which is presumably ruled out by the stained glass windows, or the Catholic Church, which is also ruled out as just indicated. But both are potentially included in this presentation of Christianity, the Free Kirk because of the psalm singing at the end and because of Howie's puritanism (of which more below), and Catholicism in a comment in the mainland scene (also to be discussed).[14]

In that opening scene of the director's cut Howie is immediately established as authoritarian and dogmatic, traits which are presumably intended to be also associated with Christianity. The first thing we hear from him is the brusque command to a subordinate, 'Get your hair cut.' This sets him against the alternative or hippie culture of the late 1960s. The other point established very strongly in this scene (and therefore much less emphasised in the regular theatrical version of the film) is Howie's puritanism in sexual matters. It is in this context that one should note the crass joke from the two sniggering policemen about the Virgin Mary being the only woman in whom Howie is interested. Taken on its own this might suggest a Catholic context, which is, as noted above, ruled out on other grounds. We hear that he is engaged to be married but has not yet taken that step (an early indication that in the pagan context of the ending he will be suitable to be a sacrificial virgin). The main point here must certainly be the contrast between Howie's attitude – uptight, as would be said nowadays, humourless and rigid – and the attitude of the islanders – permissive at least and to

---

[14] Hardy discusses these matters in 'The Genesis of *The Wicker Man*' in this volume.

some extent promiscuous. This promiscuity is most stark in the scene in the director's cut, where a young man is presented to the landlord's daughter for sexual initiation.

For all these reasons the initial presentation of Christianity emerges as rather negative, but one has always to bear in mind that the religion is solely represented by Howie. The question of how typical he is of Christianity is left open. There is no sign, for instance, of Christianity as a religion of love and compassion. Later in the film, however, the balance changes quite considerably, as the negative nature of the pagan sacrifice, considered necessary in the world view of the islanders, emerges; Lord Summerisle marches to the killing ground with an implacable ideological conviction that has a chilling effect, while Howie goes to his undeserved death with some dignity.

These two statements in Scene 10, then, seem both to be intended to be questioned by the audience, and at the end of the day (an appropriate cliché in this context) both religions emerge negatively. Christianity, apparently the norm elsewhere in the country, appears as unattractive, and the innovative Paganism of the island emerges as terrifying. To that extent the paradoxical assertions by Howie and Summerisle mask the fact that both world views are presented negatively.

In the light of the above remarks it is appropriate to consider briefly the presentation of the law. The policeman Howie is the dominant representative of the law and it is made obvious that the law is all-important to him. It may be significant that we see him almost all of the time in uniform (rather than off-duty), until he dons the mask for the procession and thus becomes part of the rite leading to the sacrifice. This may indicate a change of role for him at this point. The law signifies very different things to an audience, both then and now. In a democratic state it represents protection, especially security for the poor and vulnerable in society. For others, especially in totalitarian states, it may simply signify dictatorial oppression. Even in democratic states it may suggest repression of alternative life-styles, a point that is relevant here.[15] Basically the

---

[15] Cf. Krzywinska, *A Skin for Dancing*, pp. 83-84, whose sympathy for the Pagan islanders' lifestyle may be symptomatic of a generation.

system of law and its enforcement ought to guarantee the continuance of civilised values, which are contradicted by such things as human sacrifice. In that sense the final scene seems logical. Human sacrifice means the death of the law.

A propos that ending, let us consider briefly its likely outcome, were the action to be continued. Such speculation might at first seem irrelevant, akin to asking the much-derided question posed by Shakespearian critic L. C. Knights, 'How many children had Lady Macbeth?' But if we have engaged in the debate, then it is relevant to reflect on the future implications of the events that have just been witnessed.[16] We surely cannot envisage here an enduring victory of the 'natural', the rural/agrarian, or the romantic/mystical over the state and over reason. Unless we subscribe to the islanders' Frazer-based views there is no reason to suppose that there will be any improvement in their lives. There are also no reasons to doubt that Summerisle himself, as Howie suggests to him, will be the next victim when the harvest fails again. Either there will be more pointless sacrifice or, more likely, the forces of the law and the state will investigate Howie's disappearance and exact their own retribution in the course of time.

Brass asserts that the climactic sacrifice affirms the Pagan belief: 'The resolution to this conflict reinforces the agrarian myth.'[17] Yet, on the contrary, the resolution proves nothing and provokes a critical reaction to the Pagan value system. Brass's argument continues in the footnotes, where he is critical of Allan Brown's thesis that the film is opposed to the romantic idea of a return to nature.[18] It is difficult to understand the reactions of those who can view the film dispassionately as a piece of pro-Pagan propaganda; they must be fuelled by a preconceived desire for an anti-authoritarian stance, a view that fails to reflect adequately the authoritarian nature of Lord Summerisle's feudal rule.

---

[16] Knights, *Explorations*, pp. 1-39.

[17] Brass, 'Reel Images of the Land (Beyond the Forest)', p. 29.

[18] Brass, 'Reel Images of the Land (Beyond the Forest)', p. 29 and note 126, pp. 52-53; Brown, *Inside 'The Wicker Man'*, p. 70.

Although the burning of the wicker man may initially, through its spectacular effect, suggest a totally closed ending, in fact on reflection one must see it as an open ending. As Bertolt Brecht suggests in the epilogue to his play *Der gute Mensch von Sezuan* (*The Good Person of Szechwan*), any real resolution of the matter just presented can only come in the minds of the audience, outside the parameters of the creative work itself.[19] The analogy with this Brechtian ending could be taken further, as Brecht's epilogue asks the audience whether we need another world, or perhaps only other gods, or no gods.

In conclusion, the success and abiding interest of the film, although superficially resting on the chilling change in the action as the hunter becomes the hunted, and on the visually stunning climax, rather resides in the exchange of ideas and attitudes along the lines discussed above. The unattractiveness of the two main characters allows us to address reasonably dispassionately the ideas being put forward and debated. The British film of the post-war period may have engaged with strongly contemporary social themes (e.g. *Room at the Top* (1959), or *Saturday Night and Sunday Morning* (1960)), but the original aspect of *The Wicker Man* seems to me to be in the conflict and contrast of ideas and the space given for discussion of them. Eric Bentley, in a study of modern drama, once suggested that the modern theatre was essentially a drama of ideas.[20] *The Wicker Man* might be argued to be the equivalent in film. This is not to suggest that one is dealing here with a film of profound philosophical insights; but it is nonetheless one that, through a contrast of equally problematic points of view, stimulates our thoughts about what values we hold, and therefore about how we might conduct our lives.

---

[19]   Brecht, *Der Gute Mensch von Sezuan*, pp. 278-79. English translation in *Bertolt Brecht, Collected Plays 6*, p. 109.

[20]   Bentley, *The Playwright as Thinker*, pp. 8-22 and pp. 232-57.

Bibliography

Bentley, E., *The Playwright as Thinker*, 3rd ed (Cleveland/New York: Meridian, 1964).

Blécourt, W. de, *Witchcraft and Magic in Europe: The twentieth century*, Athlone History of Witchcraft 6 (London: Athlone, 1999).

Brass, T., 'Reel Images of the Land (Beyond the Forest): Film and the Agrarian Myth', *The Journal of Peasant Studies*, 28 (2001), pp. 1-56.

Brecht, B., *Der Gute Mensch von Sezuan*, in *Werke. Stücke 6*, ed. Klaus-Detlef Müller (Berliner und Frankfurter Ausgabe, Berlin/Weimar: Aufbau Verlag and Frankfurt: Suhrkamp Verlag, 1989).

_____, *The Good Person of Szechwan*, trans. J. Willett and R. Manheim, in *Bertolt Brecht, Collected Plays* Vol 6 (London: Methuen, 1985).

Brown, A, *Inside 'The Wicker Man': The morbid ingenuities* (London: Sidgwick and Jackson, 2000).

Eliot, T. S., 'The Waste Land' (1922), *Collected Poems 1909-1962* (London: Faber, 1963).

Ellis, P. B., *The Druids* (London: Constable, 1994).

Frazer, J., *The Golden Bough*, 3rd ed (London: Macmillan, 1913-15).

Frazer, J. and Temple, R., *The Illustrated Golden Bough* (London: Batsford, 1996).

Gardner, G., *A Goddess Arrives* (London: Arthur Stockwell, 1941).

Gardner, G. and Murray, M., *Witchcraft Today* (London: Rider, 1954).

Gibson, A. and Simpson, D., eds., *Prehistoric Ritual and Religion* (Stroud: Sutton Publishing, 1998).

Hardy, R. (Director), *The Wicker Man – Special Edition Director's Cut* (Canal+, [1973] 2002).

Hutton, R., *The Pagan Religions of the Ancient British Isles* (Oxford: Blackwell, 1991).

Jones, M., 'Now a Major Motion Picture?', *'The Wicker Man': Film and Cultural Studies Perspectives*, ed. B. Franks, S. Harper, J. Murray and L. Stevenson (Dumfries: University of Glasgow Crichton Publications, 2005).

Knights, L. C., 'How Many Children had Lady Macbeth?', *Explorations* (London: Chatto and Windus, 1946), pp. 1-39.

Krzywinska, T., *A Skin for Dancing: Possession, witchcraft and voodoo in film* (Trowbridge: Flicks Books, 2000).

Murray, M., *The Witch Cult in Western Europe* (Oxford: Clarendon, 1921).

_____, *The Divine King in England* (London: Faber, 1954).

Piggott, S., *The Druids* (Harmondsworth: Penguin, 1974).

Weston, J. L., *From Ritual to Romance* (Cambridge: Cambridge University Press, 1920).

The Wicca Woman: Gender, sexuality and religion in *The Wicker Man*

Brigid Cherry

LONG CONSIDERED ONE of the cult classics of British cinema, *The Wicker Man* is popular with UK-based fans of the horror genre. In a study of female horror film fans, a number of the participants named *The Wicker Man* as one of their ten favourite horror films.[1] Although the film did not figure amongst the ten most favourite overall, and the percentage of participants naming the film was relatively small (6%, or 6 out of 107 participants), it appeared in position 32 out of 336 titles listed in total. Given the film's cult status, it was therefore considered suitable for further analysis in the context of its reception and interpretation by female fans. Whilst the preferences of the majority of female fans are not specifically correlated with feminine generic forms or positioned with respect to feminine subjectivity, the tastes of this audience segment are orientated principally around representations of firstly, strong characters – often female, though these may also be male – and secondly, monsters of human-like or attractive appearance. Furthermore, a strong correlation exists between a taste for horror cinema and interests in the paranormal and alternative belief systems. In particular, there is a strong interest amongst the participants in Pagan subjects including Wicca and witchcraft: 61% of all participants state an interest in Wicca or other Pagan belief systems, whilst 10% claim to be active in this area. It is in this sense that the title of the paper refers to the Wicca woman; as viewer, rather than as any specific character or aspect of the text (though there is no intent to link

---

[1]   Cherry, 'Refusing to Refuse to Look'.

Paganism with a liking for horror). Interrogating the representations of gender and religion which occupy positions at the heart of *The Wicker Man*, as well as the iconography and characterisation of both feminine sexuality and monstrosity, may however account for the subversive pleasures the film offers – particularly for these female fans.

It is interesting to note from the findings outlined above that horror fans do consider the film to be a notable example of the genre. Whilst it is indisputable that the film is classifiable as a cult (it certainly bears many of the hallmarks of that quasi-generic label, as well as a cult fan following), its location vis-à-vis horror cinema might appear to be rather more problematical. It is neither a morality tale which might be said to gender socialise its teen audience, as the slasher film is, for example,[2] nor does it share the concern of body horror and vampire cinema with aberrant sexual practice rendered through metaphors of disease and contagion. Nor does it fit the mould of Hammer Horror, as Anthony Shaffer himself has stated,[3] or even bear much surface resemblance to Hammer productions. Nevertheless, some viewers do find the film horrific and consider the film to be an example of the horror genre; as one fan (a psychiatric nurse in her late 30s) states:

> I can honestly say that this is one of the most frightening films I have ever seen. The villagers are bizarrely and creepily backward and the plot is cleverly constructed so that the final twist comes as a genuine surprise.

It is important, then, to position the film with respect to horror cinema and approach it from a theoretical angle which encompasses previous discussions of the horror genre. In the popular media, the film has been claimed by *Empire* magazine as Britain's greatest horror film and it has been called an intellectual horror on the

---

[2]   Although *The Wicker Man* predates the slasher cycle proper, it does fall within the time frame of the precursors of the slasher such as *The Texas Chain Saw Massacre* (1974), which was made a year after *The Wicker Man*.

[3]   See the interview on the British DVD release.

nature of sacrifice (Anthony Shaffer), a fantasy with a little bit of horror (Roger Corman), and the *Citizen Kane* of horror (a newspaper review).[4] In general, the horror fans themselves outline a broad and inclusive generic definition based upon emotional affect as well as the more typical generic conventions.[5] Although *The Wicker Man* contains elements borrowed from the melodrama and the musical, it is, as several horror fans contended, a deeply disturbing film: 'being burned alive – [a] genuinely horrific concept' was one response (from an archaeologist in her early 30s). This reliance upon mode of emotional affect as a marker of horror is perhaps the key factor in its classification, at least for some viewers. In general, female horror fans who participated in this research preferred gothic, occult, supernatural and psychological forms of horror over slasher, serial killer, monster or gore films. Factors mentioned with regard to *The Wicker Man* focus on the shiver sensation and the thriller aspects, as well as the shock of the ending. One fan (a student in her early 20s) linked this to notions of realism: 'I like *The Wicker Man* because it is more realistic; the hero dies in the end.' Further, *The Wicker Man* shares, in addition to these modes of emotional affect, a number of key thematic aspects in common with the preferred forms of horror, and it is these, most notably as they are related to gender, sexuality and religion, which are explored further here.

Drawing on discussions of gender and horror provides a theoretical backdrop to these actual viewer preferences. The gendered representations typical of the horror genre – the monstrous-feminine,[6] the predatory queer sexuality of the female vampire,[7] and the subversive affinity between monster and female victim codified through 'the look'[8] – are disrupted in *The Wicker Man*. It is these very plays

---

4 All of these quotations are taken from the documentary *The Wicker Man Enigma* on the British DVD release.

5 For a fuller account of fan definitions of genre, see Cherry, 'Refusing to Look', or Jancovich, *Rational Fears*.

6 Creed, *The Monstrous-Feminine*.

7 Case, 'Tracking the Vampire'.

8 Williams, 'When the Woman Looks'.

with the usual generic conventions which appeal to and interest the female fans, and the focus here is on how these disruptions contribute to their viewing pleasure.

Aspects of feminine sexuality and the monstrous-feminine can be seen in *The Wicker Man*'s concern with good and evil framed within the narrative focus on religion. A theme that is commonly found within the horror genre, and that has been clearly identified (in the Hammer films of the time, for example, by Hutchings[9]), is sexual repression. In *The Wicker Man*, though, this theme is neither straightforward nor unproblematical. *The Wicker Man*, like many horror films, explicitly links sex and death, but unlike the typical horror film, it reverses the usual balance of the equation such that it is the denial of sex that results in death. This is framed, however, within the images of overt and unrepressed sexuality, the permission of which is a central tenet of the alternative religious doctrine practised by the Summerislanders.

In its linking of sex and death, then, *The Wicker Man* disturbs the conventions familiar to us from much of horror cinema, yet at the same time codes the predatory sexuality of the Paganised belief system as a form of monstrosity in general and the monstrous-feminine in particular. These themes are presented in opposition to the Christian leaning towards sexual repression and the refusal of sex outside of marriage (which appears to be central to Howie's faith and certainly accords with his position as a significant figure of a traditional patriarchal culture). Furthermore, this aligns him, significantly, with a feminine position typical of the genre. It is most frequently women who, in the horror film, must remain chaste in order to avoid the punishment associated with sexual activity (as in the slasher film). Moreover, female roles in the genre often divide along lines of active and passive sexuality – just as Lucy must die having been willingly seduced by Dracula, whilst Mina who remains pure of heart is redeemed. It is Howie who stands in for the passive female role in *The Wicker Man* (his fiancée Mary is firmly established as belonging to patriarchy but she does not appear in the film). In

---

[9]   Hutchings, *Hammer and Beyond*.

contrast to the feminised Howie, the main female characters in *The Wicker Man* are sexually active, even predatory. Willow is equated with Aphrodite and offers sexual initiation to the young men of the island; Miss Rose openly discusses the sexual dimension of the May Day rites with her pupils and lounges seductively at the foot of Lord Summerisle's piano. The Pagan culture as depicted here is both coded as feminine and highly eroticised. This, then, is a key opposition in the film and one which is played out further in the rural versus mainland antithesis of the narrative, and focused around the Christian-male/Pagan-female dichotomy.

This religious and gendered opposition is complicated further by the fact that *The Wicker Man*, in keeping with the conventions of the rural horror film, explicitly equates an isolated community with corruption and depravity, if not evil. The urban-rural conflict is an established narrative trope of the horror genre. In *Men, Women and Chainsaws*, Carol Clover sketches out the placing of urban characters into a rural environment in which the social rules and norms to which they are accustomed no longer apply.[10]

Unlike the typical rural horror film, however, *The Wicker Man* depicts neither a confrontation between the urban sophisticate and the degenerate country savage, as *Deliverance* (1972) does, for example, nor is it a teen slasher like *The Texas Chain Saw Massacre* (1974) where vulnerable youth is pitted against an amoral masked killer. Rather, it is an encounter between religious doctrines in which the themes of sex and death as outlined above are presented within the framework of an oppositional Pagan culture at odds with established Christianity. And just as the sex and death equation is reversed, so too the urban/rural character opposition is turned on its head. Here the naive police officer (a rural character himself, albeit from the civilised mainland) meets the provincial yet cultured laird (a representation of urbanity courtesy of the star persona of Christopher Lee). Although the outsider here is not from a higher urban status or class as are the interlopers into the rural idyll in *The Texas Chain Saw Massacre* (1974), *Deliverance* (1972), and

---

[10]   Clover, *Men, Women and Chainsaws*, pp. 124-37.

the more recent *The Blair Witch Project* (1999), his coming from
the mainland, as well as his status as an officer of the law and as a
Christian, are acknowledged, if not respected, as indications of
authority and status by the rural community he wanders into
unaware.[11] It is significant and notable that his origins on the mainland are a mark of attachment or belonging which unites him with
a civic culture. In this respect, landscape becomes a lesson in the
cultural geography of 'comparative religion' (to borrow a phrase
from Miss Rose).

We see, for example, that in travelling to Summerisle to investigate the supposed crime, Howie has to traverse a significant geo-
graphical barrier: the sea. In this way, he leaves all contact with law
and religion, the institutions of civilised society, behind, travelling
not by boat, but by plane. As a policeman, an officer of the law, he
is thus literally and metaphorically above the rural culture. He
passes over, rather than travels through or across, the landscape.
More significantly, the seaplane cannot cross the actual boundary
between sea and land; when he arrives at Summerisle, Howie has
to rely on the harbour-master to bring him ashore in the rowing
boat. Here, he has his first confrontation with the rural community
and is confounded for the first time. The plane thus represents
Howie's civilisation (which over-flies but cannot overcome the
wilderness) and it must be abandoned before he can enter the rural
community. It is at this point that, like other city dwellers in the
rural-urban horror film, he starts to lose his way.

In the opening credits, Howie examines his map as he overflies,
firstly, the (masculine) crags and barren rocks of the islands and
then, as he reaches his destination, the (feminine) lush vegetation
and blossoming orchards of Summerisle.[12] Ultimately, the map
proves to be an empty sign and, although (or perhaps because) we

---

[11] Similar themes can be identified in *The Serpent and the Rainbow* (1988),
though the focus in this film is transposed onto questions of race as much
as religion.

[12] It is perhaps not insignificant here that the change in landscape is mirrored
in the musical change from the mournful title song to the upbeat and
melodic fertility song 'Corn Rigs'.

never see the map again in the film, it suggests an important dimension which is now discussed in more detail.

The loss of bearings is frequently used as a narrative device in the cult horror film; in *The Rocky Horror Picture Show* (1975), for example, Brad and Janet take a wrong turn in the rain. Howie's map, like the map in *The Blair Witch Project* which Josh discards, proves useless. He needs the map to find his way to the island, but once there he is literally and figuratively lost. Once he comes ashore, he is confused by the lie of the cultural landscape and he loses his way. All the familiar landmarks are present (the harbour, the church, the pub, the post office), but on Summerisle they signify a cultural, and more importantly gendered, change. In its return from Christian to pagan roots, the cultural contours are no longer familiar to Howie. Through the depiction of pre-Christian western traditions of folklore and eroticised ritual – principally the fertility rites and the hedonistic practices associated with these – as well as the sacrifice, rural culture is represented as both savage and sexually liberated. In contrast, as the Christian outsider, Howie is the perfect example of repressed sexuality and therefore can no longer read the map correctly. In the fertility symbols that dominate the iconography of the film, and not least in the maypole, the naked fire dancing and the corn dollies, Howie no longer has access to the familiar co-ordinates. Here again, connections with the horror genre are significant. As Tanya Krzywinska asserts in *A Skin for Dancing in*, the rural setting of the British horror film is intimately linked to pre-Christian agrarian religious practices.[13]

The standards of religion, education, law and everyday life are thus absent or violated (just as they are elsewhere in the horror genre, particularly, though not exclusively, where the occult film is concerned). This is most notable with respect to religion and its signifier, the church. The church itself is in ruins, its priests long gone, its ground no longer consecrated and the graves despoiled. Howie is confused and angered by what he sees: a naked women sits astride a grave as she anoints it with her tears; another woman

---

[13] Krzywinska, *A Skin For Dancing In*, pp. 72-116.

holds forth an egg (yet another fertility symbol) as she breastfeeds a child in the ruined nave; a gravestone makes reference to the ejaculation of serpents; trees and umbilical cords are planted upon the plots; and a hare, Rowan's totemic animal spirit, has been placed in her coffin. In an act of desperation Howie breaks apart a packing case and places a makeshift cross on the ruined altar, reclaiming it for his masculine god. But this attempt to reinscribe the map with the key symbol of Christianity cannot insulate him from further confusing pointers. Howie's position of authority as a police officer is ignored and he is given no respect; at every turn he is hindered and is constantly referred to Lord Summerisle for permission – to land on the island, to look at the school register, to examine the record of deaths, to exhume Rowan's body (only the last is he actually required by law to do). Meanwhile, degeneracy, indecency and the corruption of the young (as Howie sees it) take place within the schoolroom; this itself is linked to the Pagan religion practised by the islanders, with its Wiccan spells on the blackboard and the set reading from *The Rites and Rituals of May Day*. Furthermore, the village streets and houses are a maze-like territory. There is not only a link here with the feminine in the conception of the maze as representative of female sex, but it is a clear call to the conventions of the female gothic. Along the same lines, the village shops are full of unfamiliar and, to Howie, blasphemous goods – they are both uncivilised and unchristian. The postmistress serves up fertility cakes and practises a form of folk healing (which Howie would undoubtedly label witchcraft); the chemist's shop contains a cornucopia of snake oil, foreskins and rams' heads among the apothecary's jars and bottles of preserved animals – all perhaps ingredients for a Wicca's spellcraft (and all again having references to the gothic and the uncanny). As one participant (an artist in her 30s) in the study states:

> The use of British folklore (Morris dancing, John Barleycorn, maypoles and old wive's tales) to such disturbing effect is inspired. I have always found such things both fascinating and slightly sinister and was pleased to see them presented as such in a film.

All the landmarks with which Howie is familiar are thus disrupted and corrupted, and the expectations he has of solving the alleged crime are thrown off course by the landscape's cultural and religious unfamiliarity. His outburst at Lord Summerisle is just the least sign of this; recall that he makes emphatic reference to a 'law-abiding, Christian country.' At this point it is pertinent to address aspects of Howie's character which are presented in the opening sequence of the extended version of the film. It is made clear in these scenes that Howie is heavily, perhaps overly, reliant upon the institutions of church and state, whereas women are held at arm's length. He is disapproving of graffiti claiming that Jesus Lives and Jesus Saves (the message has been spoilt by the unruly means of delivery) and regards singing and dancing on Sunday as anathema. More importantly, he is keeping himself pure for his wedding, although he has been going steady with Mary (herself linked with the virgin in the conversation between McTaggart and the postman) for two years without ever 'tickling her fancy.' In this it is clear that women are unexplored territory for Howie. When this is taken in conjunction with the representation of rural landscape in the film as gendered, the link to feminine sexuality becomes pronounced and it is clear why Howie is lost.

This is important since it may disrupt identification with Howie (which we might expect with a sophisticated urban character lost in a savage wilderness), particularly for female viewers such as the participant quoted above who likes the film because Howie does die at the end. Here, perhaps, are the beginnings of a revenge fantasy for female spectators, but more significantly, it indicates that identification is mixed and fluctuating. As the psychiatrist nurse quoted above states:

> I particularly like the way that Edward Woodward's prudish, repressed policeman gains none of our sympathy until the very end of the film when he is burnt to death in the wicker man of the title.

This in itself suggests a disturbing experience for some viewers, but also suggests that the viewer's sympathy (and indeed identification)

lies with other characters throughout most of the film. Following this argument through, it is important to consider the representations of feminine sexuality further.

The significant landmarks of Summerisle, which include the cliffs, the beach, the caves and the standing stones (there have been recent claims that circles such as that at Stonehenge represent the female sex organs), as well as the crops which make Summerisle famous, are strongly linked with the re-establishment of the 'old religion' and, through the links with sexuality and fertility, coded as feminine.[14] In this respect, the representation of femininity, indeed of the monstrous-feminine, refers as much to the rural and religious landscape as to any characters in the film. In Howie's response to the land and its people, feminine sexuality is coded as monstrous. When Howie sees the village women actively participating in sex to make the fields fertile and when he sees the girls leaping naked over the balefire, he is horrified. His discussions with Lord Summerisle on the subject horrify him further, with the introduction into the conversation of parthenogenesis, impregnation by the god of fire and virgin birth – all of which have parallels within Creed's model of the monstrous-feminine. If there is a monster as such in the film it is in the figurations of feminine sexuality through landscape and religion, and the inherent link with the Earth Mother archetype which Howie's point of view codes as the monstrous-feminine.

Moreover, in returning to the question of genre conventions, we must not forget that the point of view (the look) is central to horror cinema. We need to ask here, who looks? Certainly Howie, as an investigator looking into the murder (and thereby at the rural community as murderers, or indeed as the perpetrators of the even worse crime of sacrifice) becomes 'reluctant participant-observer' (in Christie's phrase).[15] This is made clear as he joins in the May Day parade under cover after his abortive house-to-house search for Rowan. The subject position here leads to spectator investment

---

[14]   McKie, 'The vagina monoliths'.
[15]   Christie, 'Landscape and 'Location''.

in the investigative narrative, but what does this mean for the female viewer?

The concept of landscape as both narrated and narrator is relevant here. Christie stresses that the 're-representation' of landscape in film is carried out through the control of perspective and enunciation. In this, the act of seeing (point of view) is inscribed in the filmic landscape. Howie, as the main character focus of narrative point of view, sees askew, however. As outlined above, he is not able to interpret the confusing signs in this pagan religious landscape; namely, that death is present in Arcadia, and that femininity and sexuality are inscribed into both. The landscape as narrated (seen through patriarchal Christian point of view) does not match the landscape as narrator (presenting itself as feminised Pagan space). In the heathen wilderness of Summerisle, Howie's patriarchal law, indeed his masculinity, is challenged. He is refused entry, asked for proof, denied information, and sent for permission from the laird at every turn.

It is too simplistic, however, to suggest that since Howie is the bearer of the look, the – thus feminised – landscape possesses 'to-be-looked-at-ness'.[16] Traditionally, in the horror film, it is the feminised, yet male, monster who looks at the abjectly terrified female victim. And if we see Howie's aborted return of the gaze, interrupted by his failure to read the map correctly, as mirroring (as Williams describes) the traditional horror film heroine obscuring her own gaze via a hand or arm raised across her eyes, then this too indicates his figurative femininity. Yet it must be noted here that female fans of the horror genre tend not on the whole to find pleasure in such representations of cowering femininity. Their affinity with the monster is much more complex and they identify most strongly with aberrant (or at least strong) femininity and with humanised (particularly if male and sexually attractive) monstrosity. Indeed, one participant (a temp in her 20s) expressed the opinion that

---

[16] This is a reference to Laura Mulvey's seminal diagnosis of the traditional ideological functions of women and 'Woman' in mainstream narrative cinema. See Mulvey, 'Visual Pleasure'.

Willow was a strong and active heroine who, in attempting to seduce the passive Howie, was thereby trying to save his life.[17] Although this appears to indicate an oppositional reading against the grain of the narrative – even to the extent of casting the monstrous-feminine in the role of heroine – it also suggests a possible identification with the predatory female and highlights the general tastes of the female audience in their preference for active female characters.

Significantly, other gender representations in *The Wicker Man* are not without similar complexities and contradictions. We see this clearly in the figure of Lord Summerisle, as the following quotation (from a civil servant in her late 20s) illustrates:

> The 'villain', Lord Summerisle, is like so many of Christopher Lee's characters in that he is charming, witty, sharply intelligent, suave and hospitable on the outside, yet quite obviously a calculating killer on the inside.

Indeed, many of the female fans express an interest in or attraction to Christopher Lee (the inverted commas around 'villain' underscore the suggestion of an oppositional reading and a strong desire for the character).

Furthermore, despite the patriarchal structure of lord and villagers which defines the Summerisle community, the relationship is not a straightforwardly masculine one. Lord Summerisle is strongly aligned with the feminine aspects of the Pagan culture outlined above, literally so in his case when he takes on the role of the man-woman teaser in the May Day rite. Just as Howie is figuratively feminised even as he is literally coded as a patriarchal figure of church and law enforcement, so too is Lord Summerisle – but in this, unlike Howie, he does carry the traits of the gothic (or humanised) monster. The character is both appealing to, and invites identification from, the female viewers. Another participant (a teacher in her 30s) put the inclusion of *The Wicker Man* amongst her favourites specifically down to 'Christopher Lee in a dress.' This, then, is suggestive of a

---

[17] This response is to the original version of the film which lacks the 'Sacrifice to Aphrodite' scene.

subversive affinity between monster and female subject, though like other figurations in the film, it too is complex.

The two key figures of patriarchal authority in the film are, then, figuratively female in important respects, and the eroticised ritual of the film is thereby at odds with the phallocentric narrative point of view and mode of address. The gendered difference explored above as represented through the rural landscape and its associated religions and rites, provides entry into the narrative for female horror film fans. Disruptions of the established order, which in *The Wicker Man* occur principally through its reconstructions of Pagan religion and figurations of femininity, open up a space in which the patriarchal religious culture of the puritanical Christian tradition can be confronted and resisted. The Pagan (and highly gendered) rituals – the spring rites of May Day, the folk spells of the matriarchal wise women and the revenge fantasy of the final sacrifice – can provide female viewers with the thrills and shivers they seek out in the horror genre.

In returning to the question of genre and female audience, whilst one cannot claim that the film is an example of feminist horror in any unproblematical way, it offers female audiences a number of pleasures. The representations of strong (and sexually predatory) female characters, the female-centric representations of oppositional religious culture, and cross-gender identification, as well as the appeal of the star Christopher Lee, allow entry into the narrative for the female spectator. It should be noted that whilst the viewing preferences of female fans are not always for particular kinds of horror that are coded as feminine (the female gothic or maternal melodrama), their tastes do tend towards those films which contain certain elements or generic conventions. Principally, these include aberrant femininity or sexuality, strong female protagonists and attractive monstrosity, all of which are offered up within *The Wicker Man*, although not always – as shown in the case of both masculinity and the monstrous-feminine – straightforwardly. It is the plays with the usual codes and conventions of horror cinema that seem to offer pleasures for the female viewer.

Finally, then, to return to Carol Clover's analysis of the rural

horror film, if the standards of urban life no longer apply, class status is disrupted and the country becomes a threat. In *The Wicker Man*, this is orientated most strongly around gender, both in its disruption of patriarchal law and religion, and in the threat of eroticised (and feminised) culture and landscape which it presents. Within the urban-rural horror narrative, the country takes revenge upon the city for some form of exploitation. Commonly, this is economic, cultural or ecological. Here we see this focused on the conflict of religious cultures as the practitioners of the Pagan religion take revenge upon the usurping Christianity. Unusually, then, this invites identification with the rural Other – not least in the form of the oppositional Pagan religion – which may therefore offer subversive pleasures for the female fan.

Bibliography

Case, S.-E., 'Tracking the Vampire', *Differences*, 3 (2) (1991), pp. 1-20.

Cherry, B., 'Refusing to Refuse to Look: Female Viewers of the Horror Film', *Identifying Hollywood Audiences*, ed. Richard Maltby and Melvin Stokes (London: BFI, 1999), pp. 187-203.

Christie, I., 'Landscape and 'Location': Reading Filmic Space Historically', *Rethinking History*, 4 (2) (2000), pp. 165-174.

Clover, C., *Men, Women and Chainsaws: Gender in the modern horror film* (London: BFI, 1992).

Creed, B., *The Monstrous-Feminine: Film, feminism, psychoanalysis* (London, New York: Routledge, 1993).

Hardy, R. (Director), *The Wicker Man – Special Edition Director's Cut* (Canal+, [1973] 2002).

Hutchings, P., *Hammer and Beyond: The British horror film* (Manchester: Manchester University Press, 1993).

Jancovich, M., *Rational Fears: American horror in the 1950s* (Manchester: Manchester University Press, 1996).

Krzywinska, T., *A Skin for Dancing in: Possession, witchcraft and voodoo in film* (Trowbridge: Flicks Books, 2000).

McKie, R., 'The vagina monoliths: Stonehenge was ancient sex symbol', *The Observer*, 6 July 2003, p. 7.

Mulvey, L., 'Visual Pleasure and Narrative Cinema', *Screen*, 16 (3) (1975), pp. 6-18.

Williams, L., 'When the Woman Looks', *Revision: Feminist essays in film analysis*, ed. M. A. Doane, P. Mellencamp and L. Williams (Washington, DC: American Film Institute, 1984), pp. 83-99.

'Do As Thou Wilt': Contemporary Paganism and *The Wicker Man*

Judith Higginbottom

The Wicker Man was made 21 years after the repeal of the Witchcraft Act and the emergence of Paganism as a spiritual and religious practice. Although *The Wicker Man* has not been distributed theatrically in the UK since its initial release and has, until recently, been very difficult to obtain on video or DVD, it has become a firm favourite with Pagans over the last thirty years. In this chapter I look at the portrayal of Paganism in *The Wicker Man*, examine how the film has been received by Pagan audiences, and compare *The Wicker Man* to other films with Pagan subject matter.

In the 1950s new forms of Paganism emerged as a distinct set of spiritual practices in the UK. Paganism grew from small beginnings throughout the 1960s and 1970s. As Paganism has no hierarchy, contains many different strands, and tends to resist organisation, it is difficult to quantify the number of practising Pagans in the UK. Some recent work suggests the number of those defining themselves as Pagan may even be as high as one million.[1] Paganism is now practised extensively in many countries including the USA, Canada and Australia as well as throughout Europe. Pagan organisations have also forged links with practitioners of traditional Pagan religions in Africa, Central America, South America and Australia.

---

[1]   Author's ongoing research into 2001 census returns; Pagan Federation, 2003. (The Pagan Federation is the umbrella body for Pagans in the UK and provides networking, resources and information about Paganism: BM Box 7097, London WC1N 3XX, UK).

The key tenets of contemporary Paganism are an understanding of Deity as including both female and male, a reverence for nature and sexuality, a peaceful, permissive morality and the practice of magic. It is both polytheistic and pantheistic. Paganism is a new form of spirituality, not simply a reconstruction of pre-Christian beliefs, although many Pagans draw on historic Pagan traditions.

Paganism has a number of strands, referred to by Pagans as paths. Amongst these are: Wicca (Pagan witchcraft), which was pioneered by Gerald Gardner and colleagues in the 1950s and further developed by Alex and Maxine Sanders and others in the 1960s;[2] Druidry; the Northern Tradition (the worship of the Norse deities such as Odin, Thor and Freya); and a range of individual practices based on Shamanism and related techniques. Pagans may practise their religion individually, in groups (covens, groves and hearths), or in open seasonal rituals for large numbers of people, usually at well-known sites with long traditions of Pagan worship, such as Stonehenge and Avebury.

The growth of Paganism was accelerated by the 1960s counter-culture which seized on its anarchic, anti-hierarchical potential and its critique of patriarchal monotheism. In the 1970s Paganism grew to encompass feminist spirituality based on the primacy of Goddess-worship. Its reverence for nature and commitment to ecology subsequently attracted people from the Green movement, with eco-warriors and road protestors in the 1990s identifying themselves as Pagan. The growth of Paganism has led to its recog-

---

[2] Gerald Gardner is credited with beginning the revival of Witchcraft/Wicca with the publication of *Witchcraft Today* and *The Meaning Of Witchcraft*; he actively sought media coverage for Wicca until his death in 1961. Alex and Maxine Sanders came to prominence within Wicca in the UK during the 1960s as the leaders of a new form of Wicca which eventually became known as 'Alexandrian' (to distinguish it from the established Gardnerian form). The Sanders publicised their activities and beliefs widely through press interviews and television appearances, and both had mass market paperback biographies/autobiographies published: Johns, *King of the Witches*; Sanders, *Maxine the Witch Queen*.

nition as a religion by governmental and other agencies in the UK: Pagans provide hospital and prison chaplaincy services, work with education authorities and social services providers, and take part in inter-faith groupings.

Despite the growth of Paganism, Pagans can still experience hostility related to their spiritual practices, especially from Christians who erroneously link Paganism with Satanism and/or devil worship. Pagans are at pains to point out that their religion has its roots in pre-Christian spirituality (Satan/the devil being a concept which most Pagans do not believe in), and that it is therefore very different from Satanism, which sits within a Judaeo-Christian moral and spiritual framework.

Over the last three years I have conducted informal research into the reaction of Pagan audiences to films with Pagan content/subject matter, and to *The Wicker Man* in particular. *The Wicker Man* is extremely popular with Pagan audiences. When I speak on film at Pagan events I am always asked about *The Wicker Man*, and it is clear that Pagans constitute a significant component of the film's cult audience. This is perhaps surprising given that the film concerns human sacrifice, a practice which modern Pagans would strenuously disown. So what is it that Pagan audiences recognise as positive and pleasurable in *The Wicker Man* and what is it that strikes a chord with their own beliefs?

Perhaps unexpectedly, *The Wicker Man* does not draw its narrative or imagery from Paganism as practised in the UK at the time of its making. Paganism, and Wicca in particular, had provided salacious tabloid headline-fodder since the 1950s and was the subject of sporadic moral panics. The high-profile, media-friendly activities of Gerald Gardner in the 1950s, and of Alex and Maxine Sanders in the late 1960s and early 1970s, put Wicca well and truly in the public domain.[3] Television and press coverage of the Sanders' activities, for example their appearance on the *Simon Dee Show* (a popular early evening UK television chat show), would have been

---

[3]   Gardner, *Witchcraft Today*, Gardner, *The Meaning of Witchcraft* and Sanders, *Maxine the Witch Queen*.

Fig. 1: Clockwise from top left – Abbots Bromley Horn Dancers
(Courtesy of © Eric Roy); **Rapper Sword Dancers** *(Courtesy of © Mr Leslie's Sword Dancers);*
Minehead Hobby Horse *(Courtesy of © Rosy Burke Design);*
Jack in the Green *(Courtesy of © Bristol Jack in the Green).*

Fig. 2: The Betley Window
(Courtesy of the © Victoria and Albert Museum).

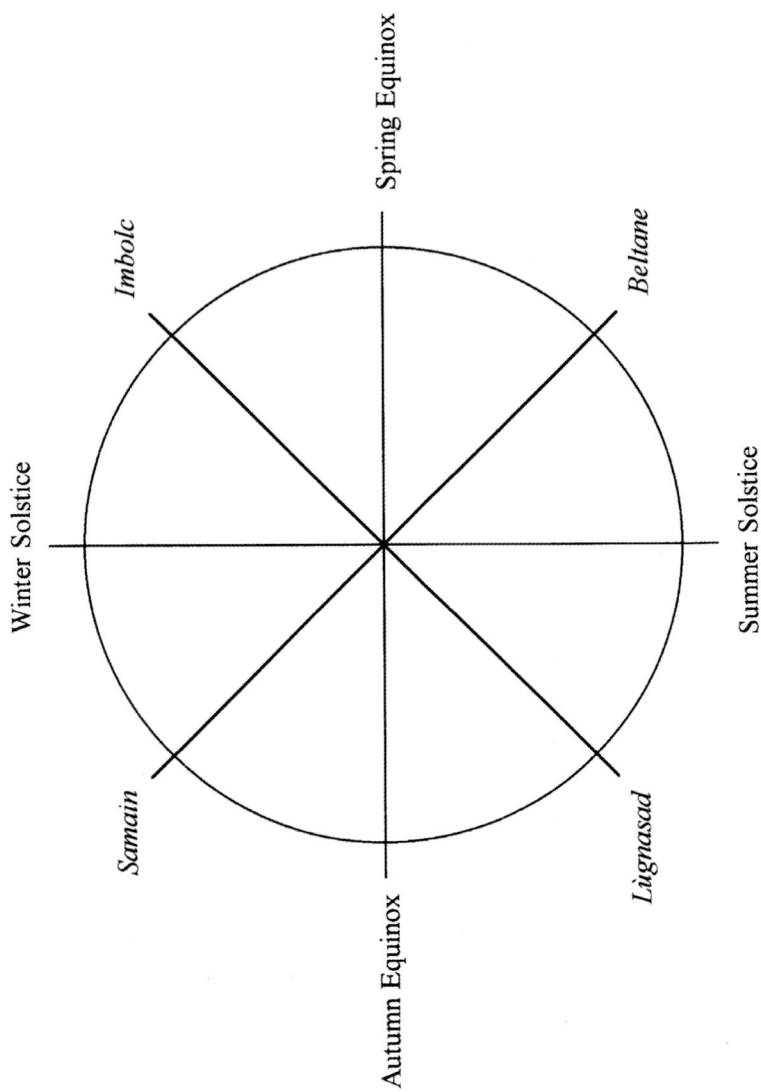

Fig. 3: Frazer's fire festivals
(Diagram by Richard Sermon).

Fig. 5: Butser Festival of Beltane, 3 May 2003

Fig. 5: Butser Festival of Beltane, 3 May 2003
(Photograph by Richard Sermon)

Fig. 5: Butser Festival of Beltane, 3 May 2003

easily available to the makers of *The Wicker Man*, had they chosen to use it.[4]

The British horror films of the 1960s and 1970s, made by companies such as Hammer, Amicus and Tigon, drew heavily on media coverage of Wicca for their source material (Alex Sanders acted as adviser on a number of horror films). In keeping with the moral context of the time, they portrayed Paganism as essentially Satanic, and located it firmly within a Judaeo-Christian moral framework. Such films were popular: *The Devil Rides Out* (1968) and *Blood On Satan's Claw* (1970) are particularly fine examples. Pagan audiences may derive ironic pleasure from these films, or find them hilarious, ridiculous and sometimes offensive.

A key point here is that these were all horror films: Paganism and witchcraft had become key elements in the horror vocabulary with which audiences had an easy familiarity. Whereas in the 1940s and 1950s witchcraft had featured as a theme in romantic comedies (*I Married A Witch*, 1942; *Bell, Book And Candle*, 1958) with portrayals of alluring female witches, by 1970 the association of Paganism and witchcraft with the horror genre was total. It is almost impossible to find a cinematic treatment of Paganism or witchcraft from this period which is anything other than a horror film. This association of Paganism with the horror genre, and especially with films targeted at teen audiences (e.g. *The Craft*, 1996), continues to the present. The subversive feminine in these horror films is not the subject of this chapter, but there is an obvious link to be drawn between it and the rejection of patriarchal monotheism and radical and explicitly sexual female spirituality espoused by Paganism from the 1960s onwards.

The makers of *The Wicker Man* have stated that the source material for the Pagan religion portrayed in the film is James Frazer's *The Golden Bough*.[5] At the heart of Frazer's Paganism is

---

[4] Alex and Maxine Sanders' appearance on the show in 1970 generated immense interest, tabloid press coverage and complaint from the religious right.

[5] Brown, *Inside 'The Wicker Man'*, p. 24-26. See the papers by Koven and Harper elsewhere in this volume.

the worship of a Great Goddess and her consort, a God who represents the fertility of the land, and who is sacrificed to ensure the success of the harvest. Many of the customs described by Frazer as survivals of pre-Christian religion clearly express an animistic, pantheistic world-view which contemporary Paganism shares. The linkage of human sexuality with the fertility of the land and the practice of sympathetic magic are obvious examples. Anyone familiar with *The Golden Bough* will recognise in *The Wicker Man* an extraordinary degree of faithfulness to the source material, one which is rare in the cinema. The Paganism portrayed in the film is agrarian, enjoyable (unless you happen to be Sergeant Howie), and characterised by sympathetic magic, sexual rites, enjoyment of the good things of life, seasonal propitiatory customs and sacrifice to maintain fertility.

Modern Paganism has drawn its inspiration from an eclectic mix of cultural traditions and reference points and whilst most modern Pagans would not espouse Frazer's theories, they have undoubtedly drawn inspiration from some of the folk customs he describes. Spiritual practices are not organised logically but evolve organically and experientially. Pagans are enthusiastic participants and spectators at surviving folk customs such as the Padstow Obby Oss, the Abbots Bromley Horn Dance and Mummers Plays, all of which are visual reference points in the May Day procession in *The Wicker Man*. Anecdotal evidence suggests that the film has increased some Pagans' interest in folk customs and thus indirectly influenced their spiritual practices.

It is very clear from individual Pagan responses to the film that a key element of *The Wicker Man*'s popularity with Pagans is its depiction of sexual rites as being central to Summerisle Paganism. Its positive, permissive attitude to sexual expression also accords very closely with the world-view of most Pagans. The 'Gently Johnny' sequence and the scene in the schoolroom are cited as specific examples of this.

I have found that it is the overall Pagan sensibility of *The Wicker Man* which impresses Pagans most. Pagans repeatedly cite *The Wicker Man* as the only film they know of in which the action

takes place in a Pagan context, where Paganism is the norm rather than a transgressive, exotic practice, and where the validity of Pagan belief is accepted. They feel at home in it. The Pagan community portrayed in *The Wicker Man* is a reversal of the everyday world in which most Pagans live, where they are always in a minority and where their beliefs can often be derided by the majority, so they enjoy *The Wicker Man* and find it an affirmatory experience.

An interesting response from some Pagans is that *The Wicker Man* is not a horror film *per se*, but rather a drama in which knowledge of Pagan spirituality is key to understanding the outcome. It is through the character of Sergeant Howie that this notion is developed. Howie's devout, sexually-repressed Christianity counterpoints and accentuates the apparently permissive, tolerant Paganism of Summerisle's inhabitants. For Pagan audiences, Howie encapsulates everything they dislike about Christianity: a repressive morality, an overwhelming insistence that he is always right, and a censorious intolerance of the beliefs of others. As the only non-Pagan on Summerisle, Howie occupies the position of a religious minority whose moral and spiritual beliefs are constantly questioned: this is a reversal of Pagans' normal experience. There is pleasure for Pagans in the ridiculing of Howie because of his minority beliefs on Summerisle, and his constantly frustrated attempts to transgress the Pagan norm.

Throughout the film Howie is offered knowledge, and at one point sexual initiation, by female characters who could save him. He cannot accept this, however, and goes blithely on to his death. It is Howie's repeated rejection of feminine wisdom (and, by extension, the concept of the Goddess which is at the heart of Pagan spirituality) which marks him out to Pagan audiences as foolish and wilfully ignorant. In order to survive, he would need to gain both sexual experience and self-knowledge. He fails to recognise, however, that the acquisition of this knowledge would render him useless as a sacrifice. Pagans seeing the film for the first time have remarked that they are not surprised by Howie's death: from a Pagan perspective it seems logical because Howie has rejected the knowledge which would enable him to escape his fate as the virgin

sacrifice. It is perhaps for this reason that Pagan audiences do not view *The Wicker Man* purely as a horror film, but rather as a drama within a Pagan context.

How does *The Wicker Man* compare with other films which have overtly Pagan subject matter? George A. Romero's *Season of the Witch* (1973), the films of Kenneth Anger, and *Night of the Demon* (1957) by Jacques Tourneur are very different films which provide interesting comparisons.

Season of the Witch (1973) by cult horror director George A. Romero is something of an oddity within the director's body of work. It was made after the successful *Night of the Living Dead* (1968), and in the same year as *The Wicker Man*. It is a very low budget film which shares the visual characteristics of Romero's earlier work, such as *Night of the Living Dead*. Originally entitled *Jack's Wife* on its US release, the films tells the story of Joanie, a depressed middle class housewife in post-1968 California who becomes a Pagan witch. It characterises witchcraft as female rebellion against the patriarchal order, and identifies the spiritual, magical realm as a refuge from stultifying domesticity. Patriarchy renders Joanie powerless in the world of the everyday and invades her dreams: she has recurring nightmares in which she is attacked in her home by a male intruder wearing a Green Man mask. Her husband is boorish, frequently absent and, it is implied, violent towards her. The film's claustrophobic domestic setting mirrors Joanie's restricted interior world.

Witchcraft becomes Joanie's means of fighting back, for it allows her to exercise power over people and events. She uses witchcraft to seduce her daughter's boyfriend, an arrogant, sexist Berkeley radical. As her commitment to witchcraft increases she takes control of her inner life. At the climax of the film Joanie kills her husband and gets away with it: thinking he is the intruder from her nightmare, she shoots him when he returns home early from a business trip. Scenes of his death are intercut with her initiation into a Wiccan coven, where she is creating a new identity for herself. At the end of the film we see Joanie moving confidently as an independent woman and witch in the outside world and making her Wiccan identity clear to the other oppressed housewives she has left behind.

What sets *Season of the Witch* apart from other 'witchcraft' films of the period is the way in which Romero utilises Wiccan source material. The scenes dealing with Wicca have a documentary appearance, and feel as if the actors are speaking verbatim the words of real Wiccans. Wiccan rituals are depicted in a non-sensationalist way. In this respect *Season of the Witch* is unique: I know of no other film which portrays Wicca in a manner its adherents would recognise as accurate, and which does not present it as exotic.

Season of the Witch is rarely seen and has seldom been written about. Romero's cult fans find it a difficult film as it is not a horror or zombie movie, and other reviewers have seen it as a feminist social satire.[6] When I have shown the film to Pagan audiences the reaction has been one of strong surprise at what they have seen as an authentic and unsensational portrayal of Wicca. For a Pagan audience, it is the way in which Joanie takes control over her inner life that enables her to overcome the restrictions patriarchy places on her. Although the narrative of *Season of the Witch* does not take place within a community where Paganism is the norm (as does *The Wicker Man*), it establishes a Pagan/Wiccan spiritual and moral framework for its central character, so that we can read her actions as consistent with this context.

Like *The Wicker Man*, *Season of the Witch* culminates in a death caused by Pagans. With both films, Pagan audiences either applaud this death or are at least ambivalent about it. They tend to read both films in a way very different from non-Pagan audiences.

Kenneth Anger's films are made from a very different starting point. Anger has not made feature films. He is a central figure in the American Underground avant-garde film movement which emerged in the mid-1940s. The corpus of short films which Anger made over 30 years from the late 1940s onwards are held in high regard by avant-garde, arthouse, gay and Pagan audiences amongst others, and have been extensively discussed by theorists of the avant-garde and gay cinema.[7] Anger's work is much more

---

6   The Internet Movie Database; peer group reviews.
7   Adams Sitney, *Visionary Film* and Hunter, *Moonchild*.

widely known than that of other avant-garde and underground film makers: in the 1960s his films became a key part of the counter-culture (largely though his association with The Rolling Stones) and are well-known amongst non-specialist audiences. Anger's work is made from a very individual viewpoint and draws its inspiration directly from his personal life.

Anger has been closely associated with OTO (Ordo Templi Orientis), the magical order led by Aleister Crowley. For Anger, his films are magical acts which are intended to work directly on the consciousness of his audience. This is most apparent in *Inauguration of the Pleasure Dome* (1954), *Scorpio Rising* (1963), *Invocation of my Demon Brother* (1969) and *Lucifer Rising* (1972). In these films, actors embodying Pagan deities act out magical rituals in which myth, symbol and complex visual effects work to alter the conscious-ness of participants and viewers. Of the films cited here, Anger's are the only ones which are made by a professed magician and which contain a Pagan standpoint, but as essentially non-narrative avant-garde works, they fulfill a very different function for their audience. Anger goes much further than *The Wicker Man*: he makes films as a magician and invites his audience to participate in them as cinematic rituals and magical acts. Although made outside the mainstream of narrative cinema, Anger's films offer a very challeng-ing and rewarding experience for audiences interested in Paganism. Pagans who would not usually be interested in avant-garde cinema are familiar with Anger's work, and have described it as both enjoyable and influential for them.

Night of the Demon (1957) presents very interesting parallels with *The Wicker Man*. An adaptation of an M. R. James short story made by an extraordinary master of low budget horror, it concerns an ultra-rational male American scientist who comes to England to investigate a 'devil cult'.[8] The cult's leader places a hex on the hero: he will be killed by a fire demon unless he can return the hex, a runic parchment, to the sender. In order to survive, the hero has to overcome his rationality and believe in the magic and Paganism he

---

8   Fujiwara, *Jacques Tourneur.*

despises. He chooses to do so and is able to defeat the hex. He does everything that Sergeant Howie cannot: he learns about the world of magic and Paganism, overcomes his rational scruples, believes in the irrational, and uses it to defeat evil and survive. Crucially, he achieves this by learning from two central female characters, whereas Howie rejects every instance of 'feminine knowledge' offered to him. Pagan audiences watching this film identify with the hero and, in screenings at which I have been present, cheer him on as he battles for his life.

The Wicker Man occupies a crucial position within the corpus of films that may be defined as 'Pagan', or as having Pagan content. Pagan audiences read films with Pagan content in a very specific way, and their reading of *The Wicker Man* differs from readings of the film by non-Pagan audiences. *The Wicker Man* offers a unique experience to Pagan audiences because its narrative takes place within a Pagan spiritual framework. Pagans have claimed ownership over *The Wicker Man* and form an important element of its cult audience.

Bibliography

Adams Sitney, P., *Visionary Film* (New York/Oxford: Oxford University Press, 1974).

Brown, A., *Inside 'The Wicker Man': The morbid ingenuities* (London: Sidgwick and Jackson, 2000).

Fujiwara, C., *Jacques Tourneur: The cinema of nightfall* (Baltimore: John Hopkins University Press, 1998).

Gardner, G., *Witchcraft Today* (London: Rider, 1954).

_____, *The Meaning of Witchcraft* (London: Aquarian Press, 1959).

Hunter, J., ed., *Moonchild: The films of Kenneth Anger* (London: Creation Books, 2001).

Hutton, R., *The Triumph Of The Moon* (Oxford: Oxford University Press, 1999).

Internet Movie Database, The, www.imdb.com [Accessed June 2004].

Johns, J., *King of the Witches* (London: Pan Books).

Romero, G. A. (Director), *Season of the Witch* (Redemption Films, 1973).

Sanders, M., *Maxine The Witch Queen* (London: Star Books, 1976).

Season of the Witch. Dir. G. A. Romero. Redemption Films. 1973.

Tourneur, J. (Director), *Night of the Demon* (Not currently in distribution, 1957).

Music and Paganism with Special Reference to *The Wicker Man*

Melvyn J. Willin

Introduction

THE RELIGION KNOWN as Neo-Paganism is becoming increasingly popular throughout the Western world. As Magliocco and Tannen put it:

> The approach of the [. . .] millennium, like each turn of the century before it, has seen an expansion of popular interest in things spiritual and occult [. . .] One of the most significant new religious movements of the 20th century is revival Witchcraft or Wicca, part of a collection of nature-centered religions known as Neo-Paganism that seeks to re-sacralize the universe by reviving and experimenting with polytheistic worship [. . .][1]

I decided to investigate the place of music within the Pagan movement generally, and *The Wicker Man* specifically, because there appeared to be a lack of knowledge about this subject in both contemporary and earlier sources. I agree with the composer Cyril Scott that: 'of all the arts, music is, from the occult standpoint, by far the most potent; so potent indeed that it has been instrumental in moulding thought and morals, influencing its sister arts and even to some extent history itself.'[2] In particular, music seems to play an important role in the ritual and culture of Paganism and witchcraft:

---

[1]   Magliocco and Tannen, 'Introduction', p. 7.

[2]   Scott, *An Outline of Modern Occultism*, p. 157.

Music [. . .] ranks so high that no understanding can reach it, and exudes such a power that dominates everything and of which nobody can give himself an account. Religious cults can therefore not dispense with it; it is one of the best means to have a miraculous effect on man.[3]

This article discusses the place of music within the contemporary Pagan religion and focuses on the musical score of *The Wicker Man* in the latter part of the text. It aims to provide the reader with a greater understanding of the importance of music within Paganism and specifically within *The Wicker Man*.

Defining Paganism

The word 'Pagan' has for many years had a pejorative implication meaning 'uncouth' or 'uncivilised', but its actual root means 'rural' (from the Latin *pagus*). *The Oxford English Dictionary* defines it as coming from *Paganus*, meaning 'civilian' in contrast to 'soldier'. Christianity has generally meant the word to imply non-Christian, and therefore inferior, people or ideas; such usage of the term can be encountered among evangelical groups in the USA.

The Pagan Federation, which was founded in 1971, and is one of the most important governing and guiding bodies of the movement, describes Paganism as follows:

Paganism is a spiritual way of life which has its roots in the ancient nature religions of the world. It is principally rooted in the old religions of Europe, though some adherents also find great worth in the indigenous beliefs of other countries. Such belief in the sacredness of all things can be found world-wide. Pagans see this as their heritage, and retain the beliefs and values of their ancestors in forms adapted to suit modern life. We celebrate the sanctity of Nature, revering the Divine in all things; the vast, unknowable spirit that runs through the universe, both seen and unseen.

Pagans honour the Divine in all its aspects, whether male or female, as part of the sacred whole [. . .] The woods and open

---

3   Neubauer, 'Emancipation', p. 163.

spaces of the land, home to wild animals and birds are cherished. Paganism stresses personal spiritual experience [. . .] Our rites help us harmonise with the natural cycles, and so they are often held at the turning points of the seasons, at the phases of the moon and sun, and at times of transition in our lives.

There is a great variety of traditions within the broad spectrum of Paganism [. . .] Some Pagans follow multiple Gods and Goddesses [. . .] others focus on a single Life Force of no specific gender; yet others devote themselves to a cosmic couple [. . .] From other faiths and from society generally, we ask only tolerance.[4]

Paganism might therefore be thought of as a 'blanket' title that encompasses such religions as witchcraft (or Wicca), Druidism, shamanism, Odinism, etc. Each of these has its own rites, beliefs and rituals, but they all share a reverence for nature and a lack of belief in monotheism. The term is modern in so far as there is no evidence for ancient races actually referring to themselves as 'Pagans'; indeed, there has always been obscurity concerning its interpretation.[5]

There is no doubt that Pagan worship took place as far back as Palaeolithic times and that ancient civilisations worshipped a range of deities that were closely related to nature and fertility.[6] The Celts celebrated major seasonal festivals and Julius Caesar wrote about their priesthood of Druids. In the Roman Empire it seems that as long as the *pax Romana* was adhered to then Paganism was allowed to flourish. However, once Constantine declared Christianity to be the official religion of the Empire in 324 CE (Common Era) it was not long until this earlier toleration was overturned. During the next thousand years the old gods and goddesses of Paganism were recast as the demons and Devil of Christianity and feminine principles became subjugated under a strongly patriarchal monotheism.[7]

---

4   The Pagan Federation, *What is Paganism?*
5   Kemp and Sertori, *Practical Paganism.*
6   Crowley, *Wicca.*
7   Crowley, *Wicca.*

The basic principles of modern Paganism can be broadly summarised as follows: the religion is nature-based, believes in the equality and polarisation of the sexes, uses magic for purposes of good, and attempts to achieve spiritual and physical results, such as communication with discarnate entities and healing. Supplications are made to gods and goddesses that can be thought of as literal or archetypal.

Music and Paganism

This chapter argues that *The Wicker Man* contains music with Pagan characteristics; indeed, the members of at least one coven with which I am acquainted use music from *The Wicker Man* at certain celebrations. Before outlining some of these features, it is apposite to offer a definition of Pagan music. Magliocco and Tannen's useful observations about Pagan music are borne out by my own research:

> What is Pagan music? [. . .] Songs and lyrics that reach inside you and touch the inner depths of your soul [. . .] allows [sic] us to touch our past, hear some of the beauty heard by our ancestors [. . .] Music was ever an essential element in ancient worship [. . .] Pagans are inspired by songs from mainstream sources: pop, classical, and traditional and popular folk music.[8]

I would expand this description to include instrumental music, both acoustic and electronic, that serves inspirational or practical purposes. It is apparent from numerous conferences and gatherings throughout the country that Pagans use a very wide range of music and tend to choose their material with care. Some types of music used within Paganism are difficult to categorise because of their integration of styles from different cultures and historical periods, and as a result of this acculturation, Pagan music is always evolving. The widespread availability of a huge range of different types of music, especially after the expansion of the compact disc market, has increased access to those willing to explore alternative music.

---

[8]   Magliocco and Tannen, 'The Real Old-Time Religion', pp. 177-78.

Alongside this, traditions of musical performance have continued within the Pagan religion.

I sent a questionnaire to over 100 Pagans throughout Britain asking for details about their musical preferences. Respondents often stated that the music selected should enhance the ritual. A typical statement was that music was used 'to provide a supportive and complementary backdrop to a ritual, or it may be an intrinsic part of the ritual.' Another replied:

> During the ritual the purpose of our music is to raise energy so most of the time we're chanting. We like to fall back on chants we know, so we can focus on the sound/harmony/counterpoint and energy rather than trying to learn new words.

Another common purpose of the music was to provide 'atmosphere' or 'mood' enhancement. Answers ranged from simply stating that music set the atmosphere for a ritual to more precise definitions, such as the following:

> Mood/Mind Set: The music I choose sets the scene for my work. It tends to be instrumental to avoid the distraction of words, with a heavy rhythmic beat for ritual and soothing 'pleasing' music before and after. I vary music prior to ritual, but tend to stick to the same music during ritual. The variation is purely according to my mood.

With the mind suitably relaxed, its focus on such activities as 'path working' (whereby visualisations of scenes from nature, etc., can be entered into) and meditation is supposedly enhanced.

Another of my survey questions asked respondents whether their choice of music was influenced by the seasons, the people who were in attendance, or any other factors. Almost half the replies stressed that the season was an important factor in the choice of music. One reply stated that all the songs used were seasonally themed:

> They vary according to the season for the most part. All of our songs are seasonally based, though there are a few songs which can be sung during any season. For the opening ritual we start

with one of the 'all-season songs', and then the subsequent songs are seasonal.

In addition to the seasons, respondents described the nature of the event or ritual as an important factor determining music choice. For instance, moon rituals, handfastings (renewals of vows) and other rites of passage were all described as requiring different types of music. Overall, therefore, it is clear that Pagans give significant thought to the music chosen at their gatherings; they aim to stimulate the mind with reference to seasons, events and the practicalities of performance.

The impacts of music on living organisms have been studied by numerous scholars of the psychology of music.[9] Ralls-MacLeod states concisely: 'many cultures have believed music to have a profound effect on humans [...] From Pythagoras to the Romantics, music was perceived to have a role which far surpassed its modern status as mere 'entertainment' or art form.'[10] My own study suggests that one of the impacts of music is its binding effect on groups. For instance, one high priestess commented that music 'serves to unite the people present plus it gives a single focus for everyone present.' This unifying effect was also extended to spirits and other entities variously referred to as 'gods', 'ancestors', etc.; indeed, music was also said to enhance spirit contact and it was termed 'a gift from the gods' and a 'gift for the gods'.

Furthermore, the survey yielded many references to 'altered states of consciousness', 'trance' inducement, 'meditation' and accessing the right side of the brain (questionably thought to contain the psychic and emotional side of the human character). Altered states of mind are studied in many disciplines, including parapsychology and musicology, yet are not fully understood by 'hard' science. These phenomena include telepathy (mind to mind communication) and other types of extra sensory perception.[11] A respondent commented:

---

[9] Schoen, *The Effects of Music*; Critchley and Henson, *Music and the Brain*; Storr, *Music and the Mind*.

[10] Ralls-MacLeod, *Music and the Celtic Otherworld*, p. 3.

[11] Willin, 'Paramusicology'.

> During [the ritual] – power raising [. . .] can induce a trance effect
> or affect the psyche of the individual. [It] can open doorways and
> bond us with the ancestors. I feel that, whilst music is not essential,
> in many cases it enhances the ritual.

Pagans and witches use a wide variety of music, including folk and classical, but the most popular category of recorded music would seem to be what is generally called New Age. Pagans also enjoy the Neo-Celtic music of artists such as Clannad and Loreena McKennitt. The album *The Dark Night of the Soul* by McKennitt contains three tracks ('Greensleeves', 'Huron 'Beltane' Fire Dance' and 'All Souls Night'), each of which possesses one or more Pagan-friendly musical trait such as modal harmony, concordant melody and rhythmic regularity. Other common New Age tropes include the use of sounds from the natural environment (bird songs, the sea, forests, etc.) and themes such as the cosmos, mythology, magic, mystery and the occult. Many folk and New Age songs refer to subjects consistent with Pagan interests: for instance, 'The Cutty Wren' contains symbolism which is closely allied to mythological and religious modes of thought, and further Pagan connections can be found in the folk songs 'The Two Brothers', 'Edward' and 'The Padstow May Song'.

Other forms of music may feature in Pagan gatherings. Although jazz and avant-garde music is almost totally absent from such events, rock and pop music is occasionally listened to before and after ceremonies. The questionnaire responses featured occasional mentions of popular performers, such as The Beatles and Pink Floyd, but the musicians were mostly firmly outside of general public acquaintance. There are several possible reasons for this. Being part of a minority religion encourages Pagans and witches to seek out music that caters for their own practical or spiritual needs. Like many minorities, be they religious or political, Pagans tend to feel that they are somewhat special, and they therefore need distinctive music with which to associate.

Pagans frequently draw comparisons between their ancient, traditional roots and their contemporary forms of worship – erroneously, if one believes Hutton in *The Triumph of the Moon*. It is

therefore not surprising that they employ medieval and traditional-sounding music in order to enhance this perception and legitimise their heritage. Consequently, the music of ethnic groups that respondents perceive to have deep-rooted traditions, such as the Native American Indians, are used for such purposes.

Live music, as practised by Pagans, is mainly in the form of chants or percussion, particularly drumming, during rituals. The words of the chants reflect the nature of the event and may be pre-determined or composed/improvised by the ceremonial leader. Before and after such rituals the music produced is determined by the ability and preferences of those present and as such has an impromptu character.

In both live and recorded music, discordant harmony is mainly shunned by Pagans and atonality is entirely absent. There is a preference for major/minor tonality and the use of modes and modal harmony, as found in much Neo-Celtic and folk music. Many of the chants' harmonisations are very plain, often in 4ths and 5ths, suggesting an antique style (the 'organum' of early medieval music) that predates Western key-based tonality. Pagans may find this significant since they often stress the pre-Christian origin of their religion.

In some ways the Pagan approach to music is similar to that of Christianity. Before a ritual (service), background music is played to set the scene. The music selected will be appropriate to the occasion, e.g. Christmas/Yule or marriage/handfasting. After the ritual, similarly appropriate music may also be played and this may even be live (a sing song at the vicar or Pagan priestess' house). However, during the ritual there will tend to be differences since the Christian ceremony will only punctuate the service with hymns, anthems, etc., whereas the Pagan equivalent may well have background music throughout the proceedings. Within Paganism, it is used at specific times for raising energy, achieving altered states of consciousness, focusing the mind, and dancing. The music shares one important attribute with its Christian equivalent: at its best, it will heighten the consciousness of the listeners or performers, allowing them to communicate more directly with, and gain spiritual nourishment from, whichever deity they seek.

The Wicker Man

The American composer and arranger Paul Giovanni, who died in the late 1970s, wrote the music for *The Wicker Man*, and it was his only film score. The press material prepared by *The Wicker Man*'s American theatrical distributors in 1977 described the music as follows:

> The music for *The Wicker Man* is based heavily on actual songs and music that are part of the folk tradition of Scotland. Giovanni attempted to prepare music that would sound like a small, town band might have orchestrated for themselves, and thus, be able to play. There was an attempt on his part not to write traditional film mood music. Some of the songs are re-writings of existing songs, to make them more specific to the subject matter, in one instance combining three old lyrics into one with some editing. The title song 'Corn Rigs and Barley Rigs' is a piece of Gaelic mouth music, on one of Robert Burn's [sic] 'songs' set to music.[12]

The original soundtrack of music and effects (forty-two minutes and forty-seven seconds) was released in the late 1970s with 27 tracks, but the track 'Gently Johnny' was omitted since it did not appear on the version of the film from which the music was copied.[13] It was originally recorded at Shepperton studios, but some tracks had to be re-recorded because of their poor quality. Giovanni states that in the case of the wind band scene at the May Day procession, the substandard nature of the recording actually enhanced the film's authenticity, since a polished performance by members of the London Symphony Orchestra would not have been in keeping with the amateur nature of the supposed village band.[14] For the public house scenes involving music, students from the Royal College of Music were hired and given traditional folk instruments to play.

---

[12] Brown, *Inside 'The Wicker Man'*, pp. 34-35.

[13] On Trunk 5 030094 021624. A new re-mastered version was released in October 2002 by Silva Screen Records Ltd. FILMCD330. It includes all the music and lacks the 'roughness' of the original.

[14] Brown, *Inside 'The Wicker Man'*, p. 46.

The original cinematic release of the film opens as a seaplane flown by the police sergeant prepares to land and there is a brief musical fragment of a drone with reed pipe. Howie is informed that a letter has been received concerning a missing girl. A scene in a church with hymn singing shows Howie as a pillar of the Church community as he gives a reading and receives communion. His approach to an island on board his plane is non-diegetically accompanied by a Celtic sounding drone and vocal duo that enhances the visual scenery. The re-introduction of the drone produces a folk-like orientation that is in keeping with Pagan culture's musical ethos. As the plane lands, the music changes to a lively folk song – 'Corn Rigs and Barley Rigs' (hereafter 'Corn Rigs'). After a brief conversation with the harbourmaster and some local men, Howie sets off for the post office to interview the missing girl's mother, to the accompaniment of the same music. The sexual innuendo in the song's lyrics is an initial indication that all is not as it seems on the island.

In the pub (The Green Man) the music is of a very different nature, consisting of the re-working of an eighteenth century Public Harlot ballad, 'The Landlord's Daughter'.[15] It is a jolly, waltzing song with lewd words referring to the sexual act, and is sung by a number of men in varying states of intoxication and accompanied on acoustic instruments (concertina, violin, guitar, recorder and small drum). This scene of Pagan bacchanal is represented in a suitably humorous manner. Howie breaks up the activity and shows a photograph of the allegedly missing girl whereupon the music changes back to 'Corn Rigs', but at a slower tempo. For both his walk outside where couples are openly copulating and back in the pub where the landlord's daughter (Willow) is helping a teenage boy to lose his virginity, the music played is 'Gently Johnny'. This languorous ballad is played on a solo clarinet with flutes and recorders providing an arpeggiated accompaniment. Back in the bar it is sung by the composer (Paul Giovanni) and accompanied by a small chorus of voices and solo guitar. The tenderness of the performance encourages the audience to

---

[15]   A song with words that contain numerous sexual innuendos.

view extra-marital sex within the film as both a pleasurable and even mystical act, in contrast to Howie's belief that intercourse should be reserved for marriage, according to the dictates of the Church.

The following day, a group of young boys dances around a maypole and sings a lively song – 'In the woods there grew a tree' – that celebrates human reproduction using metaphors derived from the natural environment. The boys are accompanied by jew's harp, guitar, violin and recorders and in the nearby schoolhouse the girls beat on their desks to add percussion. The articulation of such an innocent and joyful song with images of human reproduction is unacceptable to Howie. His visit to a Christian graveyard that has been allowed to fall into disrepair is accompanied by descending scales, flutes, trumpet, recorders and harp, which create an eerie atmosphere. The mood changes once again, however, as he visits Lord Summerisle. He passes a group of naked girls leaping and dancing to a lively folk song – 'Make the baby grow' – that is accompanied by recorders and flutes and returns the mood to one of joy. The innocent jig-like quality of this music is similar to songs that contemporary Pagans often use in celebratory rituals. Although Summerisle and Howie's conversation does not receive a musical accompaniment, it contains one important line by the former, to the effect that Paganism aims 'to reverence the music, and the drama, and the rituals of the old gods; to love nature and to fear it.' Many Pagans wholeheartedly agree with Summerisle's sentiment, in contrast to other religions that either give music scant attention or, in extreme cases, ban it altogether.

After Howie exhumes what he believes to be the grave of the missing girl only to find a dead hare in it, he returns to the castle, but finds Lord Summerisle and the school mistress drunk and singing a bawdy song, with Lord Summerisle performing the accompaniment. The lewd lyrics further disorientate Howie and prepare the audience for the next significant musical episode, namely 'Willow's Song'. This particularly melodious song displays the erotic sensuality of the Pagan girl in her attempt to seduce Howie. The novelisation of the film introduces the song in provocative terms:

This insistent beat awakened a rhythm in Howie's own body that soon bewildered and enthralled him. He could detect, now, that it was not only the drum in the bar below that gave the agonizing pulse, but a knock upon the wall that divided Willow's room from his; the supple fingers that had stroked the corn-dolly so provocatively were summoning him again. The other instruments sounded the beginnings of a lovely melody and Willow started to sing:

'Heigh ho! Who is there?
No one but me, my dear.
Please come say, How do?
The things I'll give to you.

By stroke as gentle as a feather
I'll catch a rainbow from the sky
And tie the ends together.
Heigh Ho! I am here
Am I not young and fair?
Please come say, How do?
The things I'll show to you.

Would you have a wond'rous sight
The midday sun at midnight?

Fair maid, white and red,
Comb you smooth and stroke your head
How a maid can milk a bull!
And every stroke a bucketful.'[16]

The song begins with an arpeggiated instrumental introduction in B minor played on steel strung guitar, quickly joined by a violin playing tremolo (fast, repeated notes) and the sound of a drum. The drum is represented in the film by Willow banging on the wall of her bedroom, adjacent to which is her intended 'victim', Sergeant Howie. She starts humming and then, with the same accompaniment, repeats the song's main theme with different words. The melody is slow, sustained and concordant and uses the simplest of harmonies:

---

[16] Hardy and Shaffer, *The Wicker Man*, pp. 179-81.

A major (the main key of the song) and E minor. The second theme is more syncopated, making use of triplets across the main beat, but still in a gentle manner. The harmony changes to E minor, B minor, F sharp minor and E minor again before returning to the main theme in A major. This music is repeated to new words but with the addition of a plucked nylon-strung instrument and more prominent drumming. The sounds of Howie slamming his door shut can be heard in the following section, together with other extraneous sounds. The concluding section consists of Willow singing a descending hummed passage, which is repeated over an A major and E minor harmony, together with the sounds of her slapping the walls. A final, instrumental coda maintains the plucked strings, tremolo violin notes and drums together with a single 'bent' (distorted) electric guitar note.

The combination of a gently swaying rhythm (in four time), the lyrical melody, harmonious accompaniment and well-defined drum beat can produce an almost hypnotic sensation in the listener; this accords with its diegetic position, since Howie is intended to be driven into an altered state of mind whereby he will forgo his Christian ethics and join Willow. In case he is in any doubt as to her intentions, the explicitly sexual words make them clear. It was noted earlier that the film presents Pagan values and activities in much of its content: if the joy of sex is one such attribute, then the music accompanying this scene is particularly apt.

I tried a simple experiment with a class of musicians and recorded their impressions of 'Willow's Song'. Without naming the source of the music, or providing any information about it, I played the track several times to them. Nobody remembered having ever heard the piece before. Their comments were varied but all positive and included such statements as: 'it is gentle, beautiful and rather sad'; 'is it to accompany some sort of nature-based ritual?', and 'I think it could have a trance quality if it was played in an appropriate setting.' I took these comments to be a further endorsement of the song's diegetic suitability and its Paganistic associations.

For the May Day celebrations various types of music and effects are used. First, when Howie is in the library, a brass band

is heard. Later, as animal-masked people appear at the quayside, metal strings are plucked slowly and are electronically distorted to produce a menacing sound. As the festivities are prepared, and during his search for Rowan (the missing girl), there are jigs and lively music accompanied by violin, bassoon and recorders as well as tremolo strings and guitar. A jig version of 'Baa, Baa Black Sheep' is given a humorous rendition and in contrast a slow eerie tune is played on strings and recorders when a magical 'Hand of Glory' is placed beside Howie's bed. The procession takes the form of a pavane (a stately dance) based on the traditional song 'Willy o' Winsbury' with a slow drum beat and accompanied by a wind band. At a moment of halt, six swords form a six-pointed star and each member of the procession has to place their head within it and risk being beheaded. The music performed is 'Oranges and Lemons', whose lyrics, appropriately, refer to decapitation.

In the film's denouement, Howie attempts to flee with Rowan through some caves to the rather incongruous sounds of the electric guitar. His preparation for sacrifice is accompanied by a motif of descending scales on a zither, which are followed by discordant electronic voice effects, as Howie is led to his final incarceration in the giant wicker man. As Howie sings 'The Lord is my Shepherd' (new version), the group gather around the burning effigy singing the canon 'Sumer is Icumen in' in a somewhat frenetic way, to the clamour of a wind band and bass drum. Howie's brave, solo recitation of the prayer is in dramatic contrast to the Summerislanders' communal song, which provides an illustration of the conflict between the faiths. A heraldic voluntary for trumpets then concludes the film, suggesting, ostensibly at least, the triumph of Christian martyrdom asserted by Howie.

Taken as a whole, the musical score consists mainly of quite brief pieces. The shortest is a mere 23 seconds and the longest only four minutes and four seconds. However, the music is an integral part of the film, building narrative coherence and highlighting its Pagan themes. The film's selection of mainly folk and tradional music, played on acoustic instruments, with only occasional breaks into more rock-oriented genres, corresponds with the musical forms

used in contemporary Pagan ceremonies. Moreover, despite the apparent triumph of Christianity suggested by the film's final trumpet voluntary, *The Wicker Man*'s musical score, with its use of seasonal themes and nature imagery, is in harmony with the Pagan ethos elaborated in this chapter. Thus the music, with the exception of the diegetically anachronistic electric guitar during the cave chase scene, underwrites the film's Pagan aesthetic and, by extension, supports readings of the film which are sympathetic towards Paganism, whatever the writers' intentions.

Bibliography

Brown, A., *Inside 'The Wicker Man': The morbid ingenuities* (London: Sidgwick and Jackson, 2000).

Critchley, M. and R. A. Henson, *Music and the Brain* (London: Heinemann, 1977).

Crowley, V., *Wicca* (London: Thorsons, 1996).

Flaherty, G., *Shamanism and the 18th Century* (Oxford: Princeton, 1992).

Hardy, R. and Shaffer, A., *The Wicker Man* (London: Pan Books, 2000).

Hutton, R., *The Triumph of the Moon* (Oxford: Oxford University Press, 2000).

Kemp, A. and Sertori, J., *Practical Paganism* (London: Hale, 1999).

Magliocco, S. and Tannen, H., 'The Real Old-Time Religion: Towards an Aesthetics of Neo-Pagan Song', *The Journal of the Folklore Studies Association of Canada*, 20, 1 (1998), pp. 175-201.

_____, 'Introduction', *The Journal of the Folklore Studies Association of Canada,* 20, 1 (1998) pp. 6-15.

Neubauer, J., 'Emancipation' in *Shamanism and the 18th Century*, ed. G. Flaherty (Oxford: Princeton, 1992).

Pagan Federation, The, *What is Paganism?* (London: Pagan Federation, 2001).

Ralls-MacLeod, K., *Music and the Celtic Otherworld* (Edinburgh: Polygon, 2000).

Schoen, M., *The Effects of Music* (London: Kegan Paul, 1927).

Scott, C., *An Outline of Modern Occultism* (London: Routledge, 1935).

Storr, A., *Music and the Mind* (London: HarperCollins, 1992).

Willin, M. J., 'Paramusicology' (unpublished doctoral thesis, University of Sheffield, 1999).

_____, 'Music in Pagan and Witchcraft Ritual and Culture' (unpublished doctoral thesis, University of Bristol, 2004).

Discography

McKennitt, L., *The Dark Night of the Soul*. Quinlan Road Music Ltd. QRCDP 106. 1996.

The Wicker Man (year unknown), Trunk 5 030094 021624.

The Wicker Man: The Original Soundtrack. Silva Screen Records Ltd. FILMCD330. 2002.

Wicker Man, Wicker Music

Gary Carpenter

Introduction

IN MY EARLIEST exchanges with the organisers of *The Wicker Man* conference, I expressed reservations about presenting a paper. This was largely due to a conflict I perceived between being both an 'academic' and a 'prime source'. The way we agreed that this might be resolved was that I would participate in a 'question and answer' session on the last afternoon. Happily, I was able to attend the whole conference and to enjoy the hugely imaginative and informative panels which took place prior to my own session. The enormous number of issues teased out of this strange film, and the variety of disciplines represented within the conference, evoked a number of thoughts of my own which I included within the framework of the question and answer session, and which I take the liberty of expounding here.

Music

I have written previously at some length about Paul Giovanni's score and my involvement with it and I hesitate to repeat myself here. Those interested may wish to refer to *The Wicker Man* CD liner notes, which, amongst other things, explain who the musicians were and how we all came to be involved in the film. They also feature key details about the filming of the notorious 'Willow's Song' sequence and descriptions of various working methods.[1]

---

[1]   *The Wicker Man: The Original Soundtrack.*

In the conference's question and answer session a number of questions arose about the authenticity of the songs and the song lyrics. Many of the lyrics were sourced from folk tradition and song texts written, or adapted from traditional sources, by Robert Burns. They inevitably deal with love, death and the life cycle. Peter Shaffer worked closely with Paul Giovanni and Anthony Shaffer on adapting texts into a more contemporary vernacular where this was deemed appropriate. The song melodies were original but the incidental music was often not. However, in the same way that Anthony Shaffer drew liberally on many folk and occult ideas not necessarily uniquely (or even remotely) Scottish, so too the music is of no fixed abode; it is intentionally 'pan-ethnic', as we were ever mindful not to pin down the locale. Summerisle is, after all, an Ossianic Scotland of the mind.

Sourcing the basic materials was not Giovanni's preserve alone, and a lot of traditional English and Irish music used by a group that some of the musicians and I were involved with at the time found its way into the film, most notably 'Mirie It Is' (a song roughly contemporary and philosophically consonant with 'Sumer is Icumen in') arranged for brass (the library sequence underscore), 'Drowsy Maggie' (the Irish, not the Scottish version) and 'Robertson's Rant' (one of the few unadorned traditional Scottish melodies) for the final search sequence. Other material appropriated from medieval or folk sources included 'Sumer is Icumen in' (the immolation scene), 'Oranges and Lemons' (counterpointed with a faux Scottish jig for the 'Chop Chop' sequence), the closing fanfare (Bulgarian traditional) and 'The Procession' which is a liberal re-working of a traditional Scottish tune.

Song Function

The film's incidental music, on the face of it, fulfils a traditionally non-diegetic role, i.e. it underpins action but is not part of a sound world that is audible to the characters on screen. However, all the songs (except the title song and 'Corn Rigs') serve a diegetic function (i.e. the film's characters can hear them) and it is interesting to

speculate whether this film would ever have been described as 'a musical' had not the precedent for this type of song usage been set in Bob Fosse's roughly contemporaneous *Cabaret* (1972). This is not to underplay the ingenuity with which the recurrent oscillation between diegetic and non-diegetic sound works or the subtle way in which the film slips from one mode to the other from time to time. Particularly noteworthy in this respect is the sequence in which Howie pursues the Hobby Horse. This scene is supported by a very tightly timed music cue which gives way to the on-screen violinist playing for the Courtyard gathering as Summerisle is about to address the assembled revellers. In fact, the player on screen (Ian Cutler) is the player on the soundtrack, but the solo 'diegetic' violin was, if my memory is correct, recorded on location. This is probably the most visible manifestation of the structural decision whereby the session musicians were also the 'on-screen' village musicians, ensuring that there is no discrepancy between those the film audience sees and hears. Additionally, because the instrumental timbre of the diegetic and non-diegetic musics remain broadly constant (disparities between the acoustical environment of the three recording studios used notwithstanding) the difference between the two is mitigated, so that even the non-diegetic (i.e. incidental) music feels quasi-diegetic. The unusual effect this creates is an important factor in creating the film's embracing sense of unreality, not least from Howie's point of view.

Perhaps an even more apposite example within the longer version of *The Wicker Man* illustrates how the unity of diegetic and non-diegetic music pervades the drama of the film. In the 'Gently Johnny' sequence, Ash Buchanan is ritually seduced by Willow MacGregor. This is enacted off-screen and out of view of the pubgoers but is accompanied on two layers. Layer one involves Summerisle reciting Walt Whitman's poem 'Animals' as two snails engage in their own sexual ritual; layer two involves a character in the pub (played by Paul Giovanni) singing 'Gently Johnny' whilst the pub regulars provide backing vocals and the local musicians (and the session musicians) play. Everyone looks meaningfully heavenwards at a ceiling poster beyond which Willow and Ash are audibly having sex. The song is a foreground event for the cinema

audience, but becomes 'incidental music' from Ash and Willow's perspective (or perhaps the couple's lovemaking provides the accompaniment to the song). The sequence is in any case a highly charged one: in many ways it is the heart of the film and it beggars belief that it was excised from the first release. Its impact, however, resides in the fact that we see absolutely nothing. The accumulative power of the song and the poem (not to downgrade the visuals) do much, much more than any Chereau-type erotica could ever achieve.

The Original Soundtrack

The Wicker Man original soundtrack (OST) was released in September 2002, some 30 years after the film. This has something of a history of its own that begins just after shooting finished.

As far as I am aware, British Lion, the film's production company, had no intention of releasing an OST. Paul Giovanni, however, had other ideas and he and I returned to the De Lane Lea studios to put together an LP consisting of eight tracks from the film (four per side). I have never known whether Paul paid for this himself or whether he had persuaded Peter Snell (the film's producer) to do so. As Paul was of the opinion that one or two of the film's singers – though fine within the film context – would not bear repeated armchair listening, he substituted one or two artists. The most significant of these was the substitution of Lesley Mackay for Rachel Verney in 'Willow's Song'. Lesley played Daisy in the film and sang the opening credits. This particular replacement was a blessing in another way: during the shooting period of the film this song had been mooted as a vehicle for Britt Ekland's nascent singing career and the intention was for her to record the vocal as a single, an endeavour that would have been problematic as she could not sing (this was a long time before pitch correction).

For 'The Landlord's Daughter' the vocals were recorded 'wild' with the actual actors on set. The attentive viewer will notice that not only are their singing skills dubious, but they are also completely out of time. The editing does not help much in either version of the film. For the OST Paul therefore used the original tape prepared for

the film playback (which features him singing at least one line in a Dick Van Dyke-style brogue). It has the additional benefit of being complete as Paul wrote it.

'Gently Johnny', which everyone who heard it regarded as the finest musical moment in the film, was included. We had no intimation of its removal from the final cut.

'The Tinker of Rye' had to be assembled. This song was written on location and presented to Christopher Lee and Diane Cilento to learn a couple of days before the scene was shot. I pre-recorded a (mono) piano track and this was played back through earpieces to Christopher and Diane, who were recorded as they were filmed. The piano was then mixed in during post-production and the mutilated version is what you see in the film. For the OST, we had only the voice tracks but they were the voice tracks of the complete song. Louis Austin, the music's sound engineer, lined them up on the tape machine, inserted leader tape where we guessed the piano would be, counting as best we could (we did not have the benefit of computers or click tracks). When that was done, I overlaid a completely new (stereo) piano part and after some trial and error we had a new version of the song.

Like the negative of the film, the 15ips stereo master disappeared. Luckily, something had made me insist on having a copy; this was a 7.5ips tape which was recorded simultaneously on a parallel machine and was thus a master copy. I carried this all over Europe in the bottom of a cardboard box. Then Trunk Records put out an OST.[2] This seemed to have been sourced from soundtrack tapes minus the dialogue but with sound effects. It was awful; it even spelt my name wrong. So I let it be known, via the internet, that the original stereo masters of the OST, mixed and approved by Paul Giovanni, might turn up. Silva Screen Records expressed an interest. The esteemed composer and ethno-musicologist David Fanshawe put his excellent analogue restoration hardware at my disposal and oversaw the digitisation of the master tape. You can

---

[2] *The Wicker Man: The Original Motion Picture Soundtrack, Music and Effect.*

now buy the CD (or limited edition LP if you are lucky) at all good record shops. It has additional material salvaged from various sources (cassettes of indifferent quality from the bottom of the cardboard box, mainly); a couple of tracks have been re-recorded by Czech musicians where the original was worth keeping, but was unlisten-able to in the Trunk Records version (the final trumpet fanfares in particular). Paul's innovative and advanced production skills ensured that the sound quality of the CD is outstanding; it has a presence and atmosphere all of its own. Much of what he demonstrated about studio and production technique has been of incalculable value to me to this day.

And Now

It has been fascinating to follow this film's progression from B-feature to *Don't Look Now* (1973) to cult movie. Its first appearance on BBC rated one star in the *Radio Times*; it now rates five. It is the sub-ject of conferences and TV roundtables.[3] It is constantly referenced in other films such as *Shallow Grave* (1994) and TV programmes such as *Coupling* and *The League of Gentlemen*. A musical is on the cards, as is a remake of the film with Nicolas Cage. The CD sales now exceed 10,000, which is pretty good for a small film OST whose release was delayed thirty years. I am proud to have been a part of it all.

Bibliography

Cast and Crew, BBC4, 23 March 2005.

Discography

The Wicker Man: The Original Motion Picture Soundtrack, Music and Effects (1998), Trunk Records, BARKED4CD.

The Wicker Man: The Original Soundtrack (2002), Silva Screen Records Ltd., FILMCD330.

---

[3]   *Cast and Crew.*

Interview with Robin Hardy

Jonathan Murray

The following interview is taken from a question and answer session with Robin Hardy, chaired by Jonathan Murray, at 'The Wicker Man: Readings, Rituals and Reactions' conference, 15 July 2003.

Jonathan Murray: I'm particularly interested in the judgement of Michael Deeley, the gentleman who in spring 1973 took over the helm of British Lion, the production company responsible for financing *The Wicker Man*; he said that *The Wicker Man* was one of the ten worst films that he'd ever seen. It does make you wonder what the other nine were. I know that he's disputed it since. Is that – to your knowledge – an accurate quotation?

Robin Hardy: I don't know. He didn't say it to me; he said it to Christopher Lee.[1] So I don't know whether it's an accurate quotation or not. But I think that's what he felt. You've got to remember that we were hounding him, saying, 'Why the hell aren't you distributing this properly?' Either he was going to say, 'Well, I'm prepared to spend the company's money on this in distribution', or, 'I think it's one of the worst films I ever saw, in which case I'm not

---

[1] Deeley's words, as recounted by Christopher Lee in his autobiography *Tall, Dark and Gruesome* (1977; reprinted 1997 and 1998), were: 'It's one of the ten worst films I've seen.' The relevant extract from Lee's book is reproduced as an appendix in Brown, *Inside 'The Wicker Man'*, pp. 202-04. However, while Brown's text is easily the most substantial overview of archival and original interview source material relevant to *The Wicker Man*, readers should be aware that it has attracted some censure as regards its occasional factual inaccuracies and a perceived lack of analytical rigour: see Petley, 'Review: *Inside The Wicker Man*'.

going to spend the money on distribution.' And he did much more than that; the film had won the Grand Prix de Film Fantastique at the April 1974 Third International Festival of Fantasy and Science Fiction Films in Paris; the replica model of the Wicker Man had been raised on the Croissette at Cannes during the 1974 Film Festival and caused a huge comment. And he had it pulled down and didn't show the film.[2]

Deeley believed that he had to destroy the credibility of the man whose job he was taking, which was Peter Snell. This happens all the time in the film business. Lots of films have been buried because the new incoming Chief Executive wants his own slate, and doesn't want some resounding success coming from the man he's actually forced out. That was what British Lion had done; they had forced Peter Snell out. So I think that's really what that quotation was about.[3]

It is true that the distribution people charged with selling the film had no idea what it was about: 'Lots of people dancing, religion, what is this?' They were, and most distributors are, extremely good people, kind to their children, good to their dogs, but they might just as well be running a motel. It's just a business to them. You make a comedy, and you can see it's a comedy, people fall about and laugh, and ideally there's canned laughter as well, and you can sell it as a comedy. You make a horror film, and there's got to be blood, there's got to be spooky music. But one that just has everyone singing, dancing, laughing and having sex? 'You must be mad: that's a porno film.' You can imagine the thought processes behind this. I knew the people concerned and it didn't surprise me one little bit.

But it was sent to Roger Corman, who was one of the leading B-movie producers in America, and who nurtured some of America's best directors at the time, and he thought it was terrific and he

---

2   See Brown, *Inside 'The Wicker Man'*, pp. 105-06, pp. 118-19.

3   See Brown, *Inside 'The Wicker Man'*, pp. 103-04. Bartholomew, 'The Wicker Man', pp. 38-40 details the boardroom machinations at British Lion that formed the uneasy backdrop for the film's botched UK theatrical release.

wanted to distribute it.[4] But he wasn't going to put up as much money as a tax shelter group, Beachead Properties, who became the first legal owners of the US rights to *The Wicker Man*.[5] In those days in the United States, you could get a 10:1 write-off on your taxes for putting up money for film distribution. Let's say for the sake of argument you put up $1m for the distribution, you get $10m off your taxes.[6] It's a great deal. It doesn't do much good for the Federal Revenue, I must say, and it didn't go on for that long afterwards.

But of course legally Beachead were supposed to distribute the film properly, spend money on prints and advertising and do all the normal things. They did none of these things. They showed the film once in San Diego at a drive-in in the middle of the night, and once in Atlanta – I actually saw the reports. So we sued them and I had the guys involved sent to prison. I'm not kidding. They hadn't just done it to our film, they'd done it to twenty films, and we weren't the only people who were pushing for them to be sent to 'Club Fed', as they used to call it.

So we had to start from scratch and distribute the film ourselves, which is what we did. We raised the money in the States to distribute it.[7] America was a more fruitful place to distribute the picture at the time. One has to remember that the early seventies in the UK was a time when the average suburbanite had not even been to one film a year. Films had almost disappeared. Television was remarkably good, and all the cinemas had been turned into

---

[4] See Brown, *Inside 'The Wicker Man'*, pp. 106-08; Bartholomew, 'The Wicker Man', p. 42.

[5] See Brown, *Inside 'The Wicker Man'*, pp. 127-28.

[6] In other words: a legal loophole in US fiscal laws meant that an investment in film distribution allowed the concerned parties exemption on a portion of their taxable income, to an amount potentially larger than the original sum committed to distribute the film in question.

[7] For the quixotic history of *The Wicker Man*'s US distribution, see Brown, *Inside 'The Wicker Man'*, pp. 127-47; Dobuler, '*Wicker Man* gets proper release'; Byron, 'Something Wicker This Way Comes; Byron, 'Back Talk'.

bingo halls, and the cinema was almost dead.[8] There was not a whole class of young people – as there is now – who had been through Higher Education, who had seen films, talked about films, talked about media, read books. That was a very thin layer in Britain then. Obviously, it's changed dramatically since then.

But in the United States, there were five thousand universities, which forty percent of the population were attending, with not much to do except go to movies. It was the perfect place to distribute a movie like this. We just went from city to city, avoiding New York and Los Angeles. Every time we arrived in a city, we rang up all the radio stations and the local newspapers. Every American city has nothing but media, and they all wanted to write a story, and wanted you on the radio that morning, wanted you on television. And so we went. Christopher Lee gave up almost a year of his life to do this. And the numbers kept getting bigger and bigger and bigger in *Variety* every weekend. Then finally, we really acquired courage and took the film to New York and Los Angeles and did pretty well there too, though we didn't begin to have the money to compete in that market.

As a result of that, people back in the UK – as so often happens – noticed that this film, which a few aficionados and a lot of critics had liked, was doing major business. By that time it was more than seven years after it was made, and that was in itself remarkable.

JM: I read a contemporary quote from *The Wicker Man* screen-writer, Tony Shaffer, where he refers to the early seventies film industry in this country – 'or what's left of it', he says.[9] I can't think of a less promising time to make as ambitious and, in generic terms, unclassifiable a film as *The Wicker Man*. Do you ever wonder what

---

8   Substantial critical accounts of the 1970s, commonly asserted to be – as Hardy argues here – an industrial and creative nadir for British cinema, remain comparatively few: for general contextual background on British film culture at the time of *The Wicker Man*, see Walker, *National Heroes*; Walker, *The Once and Future Film*.

9   The actual quotation, 'The film business, or what there is left of it in England – it scarcely exists – is run by people who like to play safe', is from Bartholomew, 'The Wicker Man', p. 16.

would have happened had you been working, say, twenty years earlier, with more sympathetic studios and bigger native audiences, or twenty years later, in the eighties and nineties, when there was an upsurge in British cinema again? Perhaps the film would have been more sympathetically received.

RH: I don't know. In the fifties and sixties, we still had a big film-going audience. There were still three cinema chains; cinema-going was still something people did on Friday and Saturday nights, the culture was still there. By 1970, it was almost dead in the water. So either earlier or later, it would have worked better, yes it would. But the thing to do would have simply been to have opened it in the States and not bothered to have opened it in England. It's like *Four Weddings and a Funeral* (1994). If *Four Weddings and a Funeral* had been opened here, it would have been dead, all those critics saying, 'People in fancy dress going to upper class weddings, that's a terrible thing, you can't have that'; it would have received awful reviews and the film would have been dead in the water here. Once it was a huge success in the United States, it was able to come back here, because we like things that are successful elsewhere, particularly in the US.

JM: I suppose the other thing that interests me about it is that there's a history of movies being made in Britain specifically *for* the transatlantic market, and everybody gets – well, the flip side of the coin you talk about, where something is successful in America first – these things that are made for international success, critics get quite excited here, and then they flop abroad. As you say, there were a lot of complimentary responses to *The Wicker Man* in Britain, but the response in America, it seems to me from reading the reviews, later when it opens there, is more excited and blanket in its praise for the film.[10]

---

[10] For the UK, see McGillivary, 'Review: *The Wicker Man*'; Andrews, 'Review: *The Wicker Man*'; for the US, see Safran, 'Movie Review: *The Wicker Man*'.

RH: Well, I think one has to say that the American audience was much more sophisticated then, and the reviewers were much more sophisticated. There was an appetite for film there. I mean, critics respond to what audiences feel; if you go – as we did – to see films in specific cities with the critics, they responded to the fact that they came out with an audience going, 'What was that all about?' So, I think that it was a sort of spontaneous combustion, in a way, from the critics.

JM: How did you feel about the way that the film was marketed? I know that a lot of people here will have done this: in Allan Brown's book on *The Wicker Man*, there's an appendix of contemporary reviews at the back,[11] and for people who've looked at reviews held in the British Film Institute library, I found myself very curious to see how critics in this country took to the film. When I read all those reviews, one of the first things I wrote for just about all of them was, 'He gives the plot away'; 'She gives the plot away.' I was horrified to find out about promotional posters at the time that actually had the burning wicker man on them. It's like having a poster for *Psycho* (1960) with Anthony Perkins in a ladies' wig.

RH: Well, I told you what the distribution people were like. They would have done that to *Psycho*, they were that dumb. We had – I hate to say this – very inferior people in the film industry, we really did. No-one wanted to be in the British film industry – it was a loser's game. People who remained in it were 'not quite right'. The only reason Michael Deeley and co. wanted to control British Lion was that it had other assets. They then took it public, and they made a lot of money, selling it almost immediately to EMI. They were pretty smart. They made some money out of films – no-one else was doing so – simply by using the corporate means they had. What actually happened was they made *The Italian Job* (1969) – which *was* a successful film – with Michael Caine and Noel Coward. They put the money they got from that into a building – it was one of those times that the property market was going up and down – and they

---

11 Brown, *Inside 'The Wicker Man'*, pp. 205-16.

sold the building at the top of the market. They bought the majority of the shares in British Lion at that time, and they got rid of *The Wicker Man* and fired Peter Snell. They had *Don't Look Now* (1973) – which was a successful film – and something called *The Red Pony* (1973), which was a fairly successful young person's film, and they sold the whole thing almost immediately to EMI, and got what financiers call 'a good exit'. They cashed in, and they did all that in a couple of years.[12] That's what really happened, and what the film was about, what *any* film was about didn't seem really relevant at all.

JM: This sounds like a good point to move away from these depressing, Machiavellian manoeuvrings and ask if people have questions about the movie that they would like to put to Robin.

Audience member: I'd like to ask you to tell us a little bit more about the painstaking process you went through; your part in restoring what has eventually earned the name of the 'director's cut' version of the film; your opinion of the two shorter versions that have certainly been extant in this country; and how important it was to you, personally, as a fulfilment of your vision for the project, to see that longer version put out.[13]

RH: Well, when I went to try and get the film into distribution in the United States, I found this bunch of young people who wanted to do it, because they'd read the *Cinefantastique* article.[14] I told them what the longer version was like, and they said, 'We must raise some money and must recreate that, because there's no point in distributing the shorter version if you say the longer version is so much better.' They believed me.

---

[12] See Brown, *Inside 'The Wicker Man'*, p. 104.

[13] There are currently three extant versions of *The Wicker Man* in circulation: different final cuts of 84, 96 and 102 minutes duration (the last of which is the 'director's cut' referred to by the questioner above). For further details, see Brown, *Inside 'The Wicker Man'*, pp. ix-xx; Kermode, 'A very nasty piece of work'. An April 2002 two-disc DVD release of the film by Warner Home Video contains both the shortest and longest cuts, along with a wide range of other related footage.

[14] Hardy is referring here to Bartholomew, 'The Wicker Man'.

So we then went to Mike Deeley, and we said, 'Can we please have the negative?' And we actually had a right to have the negative, because we were in the process of suing people for not distributing the thing properly, which could have come back to him, because he'd done nothing to see that it was done, and he simply said, 'There is no negative, it's been lost.' So, that was a blow. But one of the students, who has since become a very successful distributor himself,[15] contacted Roger Corman, who had received a copy of the film. He was the first person Peter Snell had sent it to. We asked Corman if he had any of the negative material, and he said, 'No, I haven't. But we might have a print. Would you like a print?' And we said 'Yes', so we got a print which had only ever been screened once.[16]

So that in effect became a negative. Of course, we had to take it five or six generations. These days, it would have been easy to do: take it to video and back again, no problem. But it was very painstaking at the time and quite expensive. We had to do it frame by frame; it was called the 'liquid gate' process. The thing had to be put through a machine called an Oxbury, and the loss of quality by the time we had been through those generations to get back to a negative is quite evident in the director's cut. You can see it's much more grainy. However, it still tells the story. So that was the film that we then went round the United States with and distributed.

Audience member: Can you cast any light on the story that the music to *Carmina Burana*[17] was going to be used as the background music before the film's composer, Paul Giovanni, got involved?

---

[15] Hardy here appears to be referring to Ron Weinberg, vice-president of Abraxas Films.

[16] See Brown, *Inside 'The Wicker Man'*, pp. 133-35; Bartholomew, 'The Wicker Man', p. 46; Byron, 'Something Wicker This Way Comes', pp. 30-31; Catterall and Wells, 'Three great horror movies were made in 1973'.

[17] The *Carmina Burana* referred to here is the (in)famous 1937 work of German composer Carl Orff (1895-1982), a musical adaptation of material from the identically-named manuscript collection of c. early 13th century Germanic poetry and song, largely comprised of satirical criticism of the contemporary Catholic Church. For further detail, see Werner, *Carl Orff*; Jones, *The Carmina Burana*.

RH: No, I can't. I can't have necessarily heard of everything. I suppose it's possible that someone talked to Peter Snell about that. But Paul Giovanni was going to be the composer from the start, as far as I was concerned. I was introduced to him by Peter Shaffer,[18] and Peter had *a lot* to do with the film, because Tony Shaffer was about to write Hitchcock's last film, *Frenzy* (1972)[19] and so he was only actually on location for about one week. And so Peter stayed – you must remember, these guys are not only very good writers, they're identical twins – and so he stayed behind and he was Tony's alter ego. Whenever I had a problem with the script, I went to him and I said, 'I think we should alter this line', and he said 'Yes' or 'No' or 'We could do this.' He was my writer, Peter was. He didn't write the original script, Tony did, but that is actually how it happened. And, of course, Peter Shaffer and Paul Giovanni were very close friends, and they were working together on the music; by that I mean that Paul was totally in charge of the music, but Peter was there to help with the lyrics.[20]

Audience member: You've explained why you chose Scotland for your location. Why specifically did you choose Galloway? Did you consider other possibilities?

RH: Well, I was looking for an island. And as you can imagine, it's very, very difficult to film an island. I mean, you've got to fly up,

---

[18] Anthony Shaffer's twin brother Peter (1926-) is himself an acclaimed playwright; many of his theatrical works have subsequently been adapted for the cinema screen, including *Equus* (1973 play, 1977 film) and *Amadeus* (1979 play, 1984 film).

[19] See Shaffer, '*The Wicker Man* and others'.

[20] Giovanni's creative contribution to *The Wicker Man*, with accompanying commentary from the composer himself, is detailed extensively in Bartholomew, 'The Wicker Man', pp. 34-36. A restored stereo version of Giovanni's original score for the film was eventually released on compact disc by Silva Screen in September 2002 (FILMCD330); for further details, see Collis, 'Up in smoke'. For critical response to this release, see Anon, 'Review: *The Wicker Man*', in *Music From The Movies*; Anon, 'Review: *The Wicker Man*', in *Film Score Monthly*.

way, way up, to see the island in one piece. And there doesn't happen to be a Summerisle – well, there is a Summerisle, there are several Summer Isles, up in the north part of the Inner Hebrides, actually – but they're quite tiny islands and I don't think anyone lives on them to speak of. Curiously enough, and one of the many curiosities, is that I understand they grow apples there. And so, we decided to use a series of locations which were fitted together to create the island.

Fitting together the architecture was quite difficult. So I chose locations, first in Plockton[21] as the kind of port part of the town, and then down in Galloway, to complete the town, to get the other parts of it that Plockton simply didn't have. Plockton is tiny, there's only about two streets. There was no castle up there that was appropriate. We used Culzean Castle and the Kennedy Castle, the name of which I always forget [Lochinch castle]. And I mixed those two, so you arrive outside Culzean, you go into Lochinch, you go into the next room in Culzean; it's a mixture.[22]

Audience member: Why did you put the bogus thanks to Lord Summerisle at the beginning when within seconds it become clear that the film is not going to be a pseudo-documentary?

RH: Well, I don't know that it's clear in a second; we obviously didn't think so at the time. I'm not sure that it's one of the best decisions we made, but it seemed like a good idea at the time.

JM: The first of many games?

RH: Well, yes, it is. It's part of the general games-playing.

Audience member: Could you say something more about your use of sources, the intellectual sources for the film? You mentioned *The*

---

[21] Plockton is a small coastal village on the north western seaboard of Scotland.

[22] The different locations in south west Scotland utilised during *The Wicker Man* shoot are discussed in Brown, *Inside 'The Wicker Man'*, pp. 31-37; see also Bartholomew, 'The Wicker Man', pp. 16-17.

Golden Bough[23] sitting by your bedside; you mentioned Cecil Sharp's books and song collections.[24] Is there a way in which you and Anthony Shaffer, self-consciously or deliberately, explicitly worked in elements from just these, or did you bring other stuff in from popular media, in particular, popular representations of witchcraft?

RH: We were looking for a story that would work as the antithesis of the 'Hammer film'.[25] There are only one or two plots in the whole of the Hammer canon. That's going to be my argument when we make the next film[26] and are accused of making another *Wicker Man*.

I suppose the other intellectual sources come from the whole background of one's reading, from one's life, really. As I explained, here were two people who could just as easily have been married,

---

[23] Within this volume contributors including Harper, Higginbottom, Koven and Sermon note the importance of Sir James Frazer's *The Golden Bough* as a source of material for the creators of *The Wicker Man*. For additional information, see Ackerman and Frazer, *J. G. Frazer* and Hardy's comments in Bartholomew, 'The Wicker Man', pp. 10-11.

[24] Key publications by the folk song collector Cecil Sharp (1854-1921) include *English Folk-Song: Some conclusions* (1907 and subsequent eds.) and *The Morris Book: A history of Morris dancing* (1907 and subsequent eds.). See Karpeles, *Cecil Sharp*; Harker, *Fakesong*.

[25] Hardy here refers to the studio whose prolific feature output between *The Curse of Frankenstein* (1957) and *To the Devil a Daughter* (1976) became, and to a significant extent still remains, synonymous with the idea of a distinctively 'British' or, perhaps more properly, 'English' horror cinema. For further details, see Hutchings, *Hammer and Beyond*; Meikle, *A History of Horrors*; Chibnall and Petley, *British Horror Cinema*. Anthony Shaffer's marked contemporary hostility to the classification of *The Wicker Man* as a 'horror film', and even worse, an identifiably *British* horror film, can be gauged from his comments contained in Bartholomew, 'The Wicker Man', p. 14.

[26] At the time of speaking in July 2003, Hardy was in the process of assembling production finance for a new feature project with the provisional title *May Day*. It is now to called Cowboys for Christ, and is due to start filming in March 2006. For further details, see The Internet Movie Database, 'Cowboys for Christ'; Bing, 'Inside Move: *Wicker* pair scotches notion of pic as remake'.

we talked and talked everyday. We worked everyday and we had common terms of reference. As I've explained, Tony wrote detective stories with Peter early in his youth, so he was very much into sending up the English detective story in all its class consciousness. For instance, *Sleuth*[27] shows a certain love for Agatha Christie's assumptions and attitudes.

I was always very interested in religion and so was Tony. His twin, Peter, wrote one of the great Christian/Pagan plays of the twentieth century, *The Royal Hunt of the Sun*.[28] I think it's one of the most brilliant things Peter ever wrote. We were very much into what Peter had written, what Peter had done. Peter was always on the horizon, producing one fantastic play every three years.

Audience member: I hesitate to ask this, because the film is so much of its own kind and is so innovative, but when you were talking about the suspense and the detective story, I was thinking about some of your casting and just wondered if we have something like the 'Hitchcock blondes' manipulating the man who thinks he's in authority and thinks he knows the narrative when he doesn't; he's being deceived.

RH: I don't think we thought about it in the Hitchcock tradition, although it's true that Tony was about to work with Hitchcock. Tippi Hedren and all those ladies. . . Perhaps we naturally thought of blondes as manipulative, I don't know.

Audience member: I suppose the other thing is that Hitchcock loved bringing menace to the small town, like in *Shadow of a Doubt* (1943). You also have a small community full of menace. It suddenly struck me: you could play an intertextual game.

---

[27] Shaffer's 1970 play, later adapted as a film starring Laurence Olivier and Michael Caine – *Sleuth* (1972).

[28] Originally produced on stage in 1964, Shaffer's play was adapted as a film starring Christopher Plummer and Robert Shaw – *The Royal Hunt of the Sun* (1969).

RH: Well, yes, the thing is, as you suggest, it's like Chinese Boxes, inside each Chinese Box, there's another Chinese Box inside another Chinese Box, and that actually is part of the whole 'game' thing.

Audience member: Can I just ask: do you feel that it is for the audience to decide what side they are on morally, that you and Anthony Shaffer weren't going to make any decisions for them?

RH: I suppose you're right, in that we feel the audience should make their decision. In other words, it would have been a work of propaganda if we'd made a film which said, 'These are bad people doing this nasty thing to this Christian', or vice versa. That doesn't mean to say that we didn't have a moral point of view personally. Personally, I'm absolutely against burning policemen.

Audience member: I wondered if it was meant to be a Faustian pact, whereby the Summerislanders had all this joy and happiness but they had this terrible secret with which they paid for it.

RH: When I wrote the book based on Tony's screenplay and our original discussions about the story,[29] it occurred to me: 'What might go on after the burning of the Man?' To see what happened in the aftermath. . . But on the whole I don't think that's a very good idea. It's much more interesting to do a variation on the theme where you see other possibilities on the theme. And that is what I hope to do in *May Day [Cowboys for Christ]*.

JM: Would it be too forward to ask if you could tell us a little bit more about your current project?

RH: Well, *May Day* could even be called *American Innocents*, which I happen to think is a very pertinent subject at the moment.

---

[29] The novelisation of *The Wicker Man*, co-authored by Hardy and Shaffer, was first published by in the US by Crown in 1978 and most recently reprinted in the UK by Pan in 2000.

American innocents may bring the world to ruin, in my view. In this particular case, it's a bit of a parable: two young Americans who are sent – rather like Mormons are, or Seventh Day Adventists – to proselytise door-to-door. They find themselves in – yes, you guessed it, Scotland – and meet Christopher Lee. . .

JM: But the great thing is, they'll have been to university, have therefore seen *The Wicker Man*, and will be in some way prepared. . .

RH: No, they haven't seen *The Wicker Man*, I don't think. They're from the Bible Belt; one is a sort of gospel singer and the other is a nice kind of cowboy figure, and they're both quite *sympathique*. But they're doomed.

Audience member: Have you already written the book of *May Day*?

RH: 'Yes' is the answer to that. And the screenplay is complete; I've been through about five versions of the screenplay. Once again, as with *The Wicker Man*, distributors say, 'What's all this dancing and singing and jokes and sex? What is this? Just tell us how we're supposed to distribute this thing!' And fortunately, some people are prepared to do just that.

What comforts me is that actors absolutely love it, and this is one of the strange things; you get actors saying, 'My God! I want to play that part', even if it's a small part. Then you know you must have got something right, if they want to play the parts. But distributors think in terms of niches. As I said, it's just an accident that they're not selling rooms in a motel, or they're not selling light bulbs. That's where their mindset is. It's not difficult to write a film that they'll love; try and write it as much like something that has already worked. Please don't do anything original.

Audience member: This is a somewhat sensitive issue, and I think it would be nice for you to set the record straight, if you felt willing to talk about it. For such a collaborative process between you and

Tony Shaffer as *The Wicker Man* represented, various journalistic accounts have subsequently talked about a falling out between you, or a parting of the ways. Sadly, Tony Shaffer is no longer with us,[30] but I wondered if you wanted to comment at all on that, in the light of the truth.

RH: In the light of the truth. . . well, I think the answer to that is, of course, many more things go on in peoples' lives other than their work. And those other things that go on can divide people, and they can have to do with all sorts of different things that happen in our lives. In this case, I could write a real drama about that, but I'm not going to.

JM: On the other hand, your relationship with Christopher Lee must be a good one. I was amazed to find out just how much time both he and you took to promote the movie in America. It's almost like an act of love.

RH: Well, it's like this with the new film: he calls me every other day, whether he's in New Zealand or wherever. Christopher is one of my favourite people, and he's very funny and a wonderful companion. The secret of his success and why he has made more films than any other living actor, I believe, is his extraordinary 'screen presence'. Try looking at another actor when Christopher is on the screen. That and his wonderful voice – which he can use to great effect in half a dozen languages.

Audience member: Do you have any ideas as to why *The Wicker Man* has been so well received in France?

RH: Well, I think it's been well received all over. Just last year, we went to two film festivals in Italy, which has a similar taste in movies, and the film was honoured with prizes and all sorts of

---

[30] Shaffer died in 2001; see Brown, *Inside 'The Wicker Man'*, pp. 59-60 for a brief discussion of the estrangement between Hardy and Shaffer.

things. In France, I think they recognised it as a *film fantastique*,[31] which is a genre which is very much their own. I think that the surprise of having Anglo-Saxons produce something like that was a shock, but a nice shock.

JM: You talk about the corporate mindset of distributors and this idea of churning things off assembly line-style. How do you feel about the prospect of a *Wicker Man* re-make?[32] Have you been consulted?

RH: I haven't been consulted at all. As I described, Deeley sold British Lion to EMI, then something like fourteen companies later, Lion was sold to Canon; finally it came down to a French company called Lumiere, which was bought by GTC, which was then part of Canal+. Canal+ is part of Vivendi. Vivendi also owns – at least they did last week, I don't know whether they do this week – Universal. So the rights to *The Wicker Man* were sold within the company because what's-his-name wanted to play Howie.

JM: Nicolas Cage?

RH: Yes. Whether they will ever do it, these things are bought all the time, for actors, stars say, 'I'd quite like to do this', but they already have a slate of three films to do, and the studio say, 'Oh sure',

---

[31] 'Fantastique', in the sense that Hardy uses the term here, refers to a French literary and film generic classification designating a loose narrative mode that variously incorporates elements of science fiction, fantasy and horror, and that juxtaposes the real with the supernatural. While not exclusively – or even predominantly – French, the *film fantastique* has, as Hardy notes, a particularly strong popular association with the cinema of that country. For further details, see Donald, *Fantasy and the Cinema*; Powrie and Reader, *French Cinema*, pp. 1-53.

[32] International film trade journal *Variety* carried a number of articles in spring 2002 detailing plans for an American studio remake of *The Wicker Man*, starring Nicolas Cage and directed by Neil La Bute, writer/director of *In The Company of Men* (1997) and *Your Friends and Neighbors* (1998). This proposed project has never yet come to fruition. See Bing, '*Wicker* Horror War Erupts'; Bing, 'Inside Move: Whither *Wicker*?'

because they want to keep stars happy, so they pay out a million dollars to buy the thing, and pay Canal+. That's what happened. Personally, I think it's a very difficult film to re-make. It's got a poisoned pill in it, almost. I wouldn't want to try and re-make it, and I'm not against re-makes – I think some re-makes are terrific and well worth seeing.

JM: Could you say something briefly about how Edward Woodward was cast, because I think Woodward was fantastic, and you regret that there weren't more quality movies coming out of Britain at the time, so you could see him in more.

RH: Well, Woodward wasn't our first choice. I'd been living in America; half the time I was away filming other things, and I had never seen *Callan*, which was a big television hit in England.[33] I'd never seen it, never seen his work. We tried Michael York for the part of Howie. We also tried David Hemmings and he wanted to do it, but he was then doing something else. So someone showed me some of the *Callan* stuff and I thought Woodward was terrific, and I thought he would be very good.[34] He meant nothing in the United States at the time (although, of course, he did later)[35] but he was a good name for the UK and so he did it. And I'm glad he did, he was wonderful.

JM: It would have been very different with Michael York. . .

---

[33] *Callan* (1967-72) was an immensely successful thriller series broadcast on British commercial television network ITV, with Woodward playing the eponymous central character, a government assassin. A spin-off feature film – *Callan* (1974) – was produced the year after *The Wicker Man*.

[34] Hardy comments further on the reasoning behind the eventual casting of Howie in Brown, *Inside 'The Wicker Man'*, p. 40.

[35] Hardy here refers to Woodward's remarkable transatlantic success in the role of Robert McCall, central character of *The Equalizer* (1985-89), an American crime series featuring the exploits of a former spy turned benign vigilante in New York City.

RH: You'd have played up innocence in the character of Michael York, more than that rectitude in Woodward. It could have worked with Michael York. I think Michael made a great mistake by not doing it, at the moment when his career really needed something which would have been special. But he was married to a lady who kind of saw him as a matinee idol, and she didn't like how he was treated in the script, didn't like his being burnt at the end, which I can understand.

JM: It only remains for me to thank you for your participation. We've thoroughly enjoyed it, and more specifically, Robin, I think it's great that you've come. . .

RH: Well, I've enjoyed it, too.

JM: May I say that we've appreciated both your film and your presence today.

RH: Thank you.

Bibliography

Ackerman, R. and Frazer, R., *J.G. Frazer: His life and work and the making of 'The Golden Bough'* (London: Palgrave MacMillan, 2001).

Andrews, N., 'Review: *The Wicker Man*', *The Financial Times*, 14 December 1973, n.p. (British Film Institute Reading Room microfiche).

Anon, 'Review: *The Wicker Man*', *Film Score Monthly*, 7.8, October 2002, pp. 45-46.

Anon, 'Review: *The Wicker Man*', *Music From The Movies*, 35/6, 2002, pp. 69-70.

Bartholomew, D., 'The Wicker Man', *Cinefantastique* 6.3, Winter 1977, pp. 4-18, pp. 32-46.

Bing, J., 'Wicker Horror War Erupts', 20 March 2002, http://www.variety.com/index.asp?layout=upsell_article& articleID=VR1117864269&cs=1 [Accessed 21 January 2005].

_____, 'Inside Move: Whither Wicker?', 26 March 2002, http://www.variety.com/index.asp?layout=upsell_article& articleID=VR1117864415&cs=1 [Accessed 21 January 2005]

_____, 'Inside Move: Wicker pair scotches notion of pic as remake', 17 April 2002, http://www.variety.com/index.asp?layout=upsell_article& articleID=VR1117865603&cs=1 [Accessed 20 January 2005].

Brown, A., Inside 'The Wicker Man': The morbid ingenuities (London: Sidgwick and Jackson, 2000).

Byron, S., 'Something Wicker This Way Comes', Film Comment 13.6, Nov/Dec 1977, pp. 29-31.

_____, 'Back Talk', Film Comment 14.2, Mar/Apr (1978), p. 78.

Catterall, A. and Wells, S., 'Three great horror movies were made in 1973', The Guardian (G2 section), 8 January 1999, pp. 10-11.

Chibnall, S. and Petley, J., eds., British Horror Cinema (London: Routledge, 2001).

Collis, C., 'Up in smoke', The Daily Telegraph (arts section), 23 May 1998, p. 1.

Dobuler, S. L., 'Wicker Man gets proper release in US after 6 years', Hollywood Reporter, 261.9, 3 April 1980, p. 1, p. 4.

Donald, J., ed., Fantasy and the Cinema (London: BFI, 1989).

Frazer, J., The Golden Bough: A study in magic and religion (Mineola, NY: Dover, 2002).

Hardy, R and Shaffer, A., The Wicker Man: A novel (London: Pan, 2000).

Harker, D., Fakesong: The manufacture of British 'folksong' (Milton Keynes: Open University Press, 1985).

Hutchings, P., Hammer and Beyond: The British horror film (Manchester: Manchester University Press, 1993).

Internet Movie Database, The, 'Cowboys for Christ', http://www.imdb.com/title/tto323808/

Jones, M. H., ed., *The Carmina Burana: Four essays* (London: King's College Centre for Late Antique and Medieval Studies, 2000).

Karpeles, M., *Cecil Sharp. His life and work* (London: Routledge, 1967).

Kermode, M., 'A very nasty piece of work', *The Independent* (review section), 21 December 2001, p. 11.

Lee, C., *Tall, Dark and Gruesome* (London: W. H. Allen, 1977).

McGillivary, D., 'Review: *The Wicker Man*', *Monthly Film Bulletin*, 41.480, January 1974, p. 16.

Meikle, D. with Koetting, C. T., *A History of Horrors: The rise and fall of Hammer* (Lanham MD/London: Scarecrow, 1996).

Petley, J., 'Review: *Inside The Wicker Man*', *Journal of Popular British Cinema*, 5, 2002, pp. 166-70.

Powrie P. and Reader, K., *French Cinema: A student's guide* (London: Arnold, 2002).

Safran, D., 'Review: *The Wicker Man*', *Hollywood Reporter*, 255.24, 20 February 1979, p. 3, p. 8.

Shaffer, A., '*The Wicker Man* and others', *Sight and Sound*, 5.8, August 1995, pp. 28-29.

Sharp, C., *English Folk-Song: Some conclusions*, 4th ed (London: Wakefield, 1972).

——, *The Morris Book: A history of Morris dancing* (London: Wakefield, 1974-5).

Walker, A., *National Heroes: British cinema in the seventies and eighties* (London: Harrap, 1985).

Walker, J., *The Once and Future Film: British cinema in the seventies and eighties* (London: Methuen, 1985).

Werner, T., *Carl Orff*, trans. V. Maschat (London: Schott, 1988).

Notes on Contributors

Gary Carpenter is a Teaching Fellow at Liverpool Institute of Performing Arts (LIPA), where he specialises in Film/TV music, Music-Theatre Studies and Music Creation. He teaches composition at the Royal Northern College of Music (Manchester) and with the National Youth Orchestra of Great Britain. He is also a widely performed concert composer. He was the associate music director for *The Wicker Man*.

Brigid Cherry lectures in Film and Television at St Mary's College, University of Surrey. Her research focuses on audiences and identity, particularly in the area of fan cultures. She has published on the female horror film audience, gender and identity in Star Wars fan fiction communities and nationality in British science fiction fandom. She has also written on vampire and Gothic cinema, Jan Svankmajer, and the films of Clive Barker.

Benjamin Franks is Lecturer in Social and Political Philosophy at the University of Glasgow, Crichton Campus in Dumfries. His book on anarchisms, *Rebel Alliances*, is due to be published by AK Press (Edinburgh) in 2006.

Robin Hardy has been the author of a number of novels – including *The Education of Don Juan* (1980) – and plays, most notably *Winnie* (1988), which opened at the Victoria Palace in London in 1988. He has also contributed journalism to *The New York Times*. As a feature filmmaker, Hardy wrote and directed *The Fantasist* (1986), based on a Patrick McGinley novel. He is the co-writer of *The Wicker* Man novel with Anthony Shaffer, and the director of the classic 1973 film of the same name.

Anthony J. Harper lectured in the Department of German at the University of Edinburgh and from 1979-95 was Professor and Head of German Studies at the University of Strathclyde, retiring in 1998. Sadly, Professor Harper died in November 2004. He was the author of numerous books and articles on German literature from 1600 to the present.

Stephen Harper is Senior Lecturer in Media Studies at the University of Portsmouth. His special interest is in media representations of mental health and gender studies. He is author of *Insanity, Individuals and Society in Late-Medieval English Literature* (Mellen, 2003) as well as several articles on media, gender and mental health.

Judith Higginbottom is Head of Production at Sgrin, the national film funding agency for Wales, where she is responsible for funding and assessing the development and production of feature films. She acts as Executive Producer on films supported through Lottery funds in Wales. Recent films supported include *The Tulse Luper Suitcases* (Peter Greenaway) and *A Way Of Life* (Amma Asante). She has worked in the film industry for twenty years and was formerly an independent film maker and artist.

Paula James was a mature student at University of Southampton where she completed a Latin degree and PhD in the Latin novel whilst also bringing up children. She has published widely in the field of Latin literature, especially Apuleius and Ovid. Paula is co-editing and authoring a collection of essays on significant and symbolic literary parrots – *Parrot Play: the Trickster in the Text* – and is researching classical themes in *Buffy the Vampire Slayer*.

Mikel J. Koven is Lecturer in Film and Television Studies at the University of Wales, Aberystwyth. He has published extensively in the area of folklore and film, including co-editing a special issue of *Western Folklore* on the subject. His work has appeared in such journals as *Literature/Film Quarterly*, *Journal of American Folklore*, *Scope*, *Folklore*, *Culture and Tradition* and *Contemporary Legend*. He is currently finishing work on a book on the Italian *giallo* film.

Donald V. L. Macleod is Minton Lecturer in Scottish Heritage and Tourism at the University of Glasgow, Crichton Campus. He has a doctorate in social anthropology from the University of Oxford and has researched in the Canary Islands, the Caribbean and Scotland, on issues concerning globalisation, development, identity, cultural change and tourism. He has taught courses on ethnographic film, travel writing and cultural heritage, as well as anthropology and tourism. His publications include: *Tourism, Globalisation and Cultural Change* (monograph); *Niche Tourism in Question* (editor); and *Tourists and Tourism* (co-editor).

Jonathan Murray teaches in the Centre for Visual and Cultural Studies at Edinburgh College of Art. He has published several scholarly articles on Scottish film culture, with a book-length Researcher's Guide to Scottish Cinema, prepared in collaboration with Scottish Screen, forthcoming in 2005. His other research interests include contemporary British cinema and twentieth century Scottish history and culture.

Luc Racaut is Lecturer in History at the University of Newcastle-upon-Tyne. He is the author of *Hatred in Print: Catholic Propaganda and Protestant Identity during the French Wars of Religion* (Ashgate, 2002). His most recent publications are 'A Protestant or Catholic Superstition? Astrology and Eschatology during the French Wars of Religion', in *Religion and Superstition in Reformation Europe*, ed. W. Naphy and H. Parish (Manchester, 2003) and 'Anglicanism and Gallicanism: Between Rome and Geneva?', *Archiv für Reformationsgeschichte*, forthcoming. His current research concerns printing and Catholic reform in sixteenth century France.

Richard Sermon is Gloucester City Archaeologist, and has a longstanding interest in both historical linguistics and English folklore. He is the author of papers on the validity of the so-called 'Celtic' calendar and the origins of wassailing.

Lesley Stevenson completed her PhD on the representation of traditional music in Scottish tourism, at the University of Glasgow in 2005. She is currently Lecturer in Tourism and Leisure at Liverpool Hope University College.

Melvyn J. Willin possesses doctorates in parapsychology and witchcraft from the perspective of music. He is currently in receipt of a university scholarship to study the parapsychological implications of witchcraft, and in his role as the Archivist to the Society for Psychical Research he is involved with the investigation and archiving of anomalous phenomena.

Index

Cowboys for Christ

Robin Hardy
ISBN 1 905222 41 6 HBK £14.99

A NOVEL OF RELIGIOUS
SEXUALITY AND PAGAN MURDER

If I am a Rabbi, Jehova is my God. If I am a Mullah, Allah the merciful is He. If a Christian, Jesus is my Lord. Millions of people worldwide worship the sun. Here in Tressock I believe the old religion of the Celts fits our needs at this time. Isn't that all you can ask of a religion?

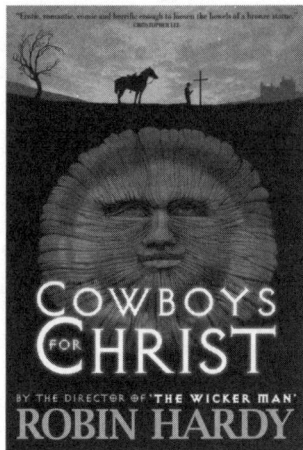

Gospel singer Beth and her cowboy boyfriend Steve, two virgins promised to each other through 'the Silver Ring Thing', set off from Texas to enlighten the Scottish heathens in the ways of Christ. When, after initial hostility, they are welcomed with joy and elation to the village of Tressock, they assume their hosts simply want to hear more about Jesus.

How innocent and wrong they are.

Cowboys for Christ inhabits the same disturbing territory as *The Wicker Man*. Ripping through the themes of religion, paganism, power, sex and sacrifice, it builds to a gruesome, excruciating climax drawn from the terrifying imagination of *The Wicker Man's* director, Robin Hardy.

'Erotic, romantic, comic and horrific enough to loosen the bowels of a bronze statue.'

CHRISTOPHER LEE

The Quest for Arthur

Stuart McHardy

ISBN 1 84282 012 5 HBK £16.99

King Arthur of Camelot and the Knights of the Round Table are enduring romantic figures. A national hero for the Bretons, the Welsh and the English alike, Arthur is a potent figure for many. This quest leads to a radical new knowledge of the ancient myth.

Historian, storyteller and folklorist Stuart McHardy believes he has uncovered the origins of this inspirational figure, the true Arthur. He incorporates knowledge of folklore and placename studies with an archaeological understanding of the sixth century.

Combining knowledge of the earliest records and histories of Arthur with an awareness of the importance of oral traditions, this quest leads to the discovery that the enigmatic origins of Arthur lie not in Brittany, England or Wales. Instead they lie in that magic land the ancient Welsh called Y Gogledd, 'The North'; the North of Britain, which we now call – Scotland.

The Quest for the Nine Maidens

Stuart McHardy

ISBN 0 946487 66 9 HBK £16.99

When King Arthur was conveyed to Avalon they were there.

When Odin summoned warriors to Valhalla they were there.

When Apollo was worshipped on Greek mountains they were there.

When Brendan came to the Island of Women they were there.

They tended the Welsh goddess Cerridwen's cauldron on inspiration, and armed the hero Peredur. They are found in Britain, Ireland, Norway, Iceland, Gaul, Greece, Africa and as far afield as South America and Oceania. They are the Nine Maidens – the priestesses of the Mother Goddess.

From the Stone Age to the twenty-first century, the Nine Maidens come in many forms – Muses, Maenads, Valkyries, seeresses and druidesses. In this book Stuart McHardy traces the Nine Maidens from both Christian and pagan sources, and begins to uncover one of the most ancient and widespread of human institutions.

The Quest for the Celtic Key

Karen Ralls-MacLeod and Ian Robertson
ISBN 1 84282 084 2 PBK £7.99

Full of mystery, magic and intrigue, Scotland's past is still burning with unanswered questions. Many of these have been asked before, some have never before been broached – but all are addressed with the inquisitiveness of true detectives in *The Quest for the Celtic Key*. This is a collaboration between medieval Celtic historian Karen Ralls-MacLeod and Scottish Masonic researcher Ian Robertson, both of whom explore and unearth with relish the little known facts embedded within early Scottish history.

Was Winston Churchill really a practising member of a Druid order?

What are the similarities between Merlin and Christ?

What is hidden in the vaults at Rosslyn Chapel?

Why is the lore surrounding Scottish freemasonry so unique?

Encompassing well-known events and personae, whilst also tackling the more obscure elements in Scottish history, *The Quest for the Celtic Key* illustrates how the seemingly disparate 'mysteries of history' are connected.

'A travelogue which enriches the mythologies and histories so beautifully told, with many newly wrought connection to places, buildings stones and other remains.'

REV. DR MICHAEL NORTHCOTT, Faculty of Divinity, University of Edinburgh

The Quest for The Original Horse Whisperers

Russell Lyon
ISBN 1 84282 020 6 HBK £16.99

Robert Redford's acclaimed film *The Horse Whisperer*, based on the bestselling novel by Nicholas Evans, heightened curiosity in modern day 'Horse Whisperers', such as American Monty Roberts.

Who were the Original Horse Whisperers? Who were the Secret Society of Horsemen?

What were the secret oaths and rituals that all new recruits had to learn to become members of the Secret Society?

Did they have a magic Word? What was the Word?

Did it work? How did it work?

How different are the Original Horse Whisperers of two hundred years ago to Modern Whisperers? Were they better? Could their methods be used today?

Russell Lyon has spent his professional life as a veterinary surgeon caring for and treating horses, which has given him a unique perspective on the methods employed by the Original Horse Whisperers. In this book he reveals much new and previously unpublished information about the Original Horse Whisperers derived from extensive research, including many letters and old notebooks sent to him following an appeal in regional newspapers.

The Golden Menagerie

Allan Cameron
ISBN 1 84282 057 5 PBK £9.99

For Lucian Heatherington-Jones, a pink-haired, punk adolescent from Croydon, his meeting with a mirth-seeking sect plunges him into a series of nightmarish metamorphoses from which he can only be saved by the wise and magnanimous (and beautiful) Fotis. Drawing on themes from ancient mythology, eschewing the expected and thoroughly engaging the reader, *The Golden Menagerie* stylishly defies our concept of the novel – and entertains.

The Golden Menagerie is part homage to and part update of *The Golden Ass* by Apuleius, in accord with modern morality. It stands Cameron in a proud literary tradition.

. . . fantastic invention and reflections on the human predicament . . . consistently fascinating and readable, the work of a writer of high intelligence who has a stylish way with words.

ERIC HOBSBAWM, historian

...a humorous, wild...critique of the human state....This is a beautiful tale...highly rewarding, in the richness, precision and humour of its language...

SCOTTISH REVIEW OF BOOKS

Highland Myths and Legends

George W Macpherson
ISBN 1 84282 064 8 PBK £5.99

The mythical, the legendary, the true – this is the stuff of stories and storytellers, the preserve of Scotland's ancient oral tradition.

Celtic heroes, fairies, Druids, selkies, sea horses, magicians, giants, Viking invaders – all feature in this collection of traditional Scottish tales, the like of which have been told around campfires for centuries and are still told today.

Drawn from storyteller George W Macpherson's extraordinary repertoire of tales and lore, each story has been passed down through generations of oral tradition – some are over 2,500 years old. Strands of these timeless tales cross over and interweave to create a delicate tapestry of Highland Scotland as depicted by its myths and legends.

I have heard George telling his stories... and it is an unforgettable experience... This is a unique book and a 'must buy'...

DALRIADA: THE JOURNAL OF CELTIC HERITAGE AND CULTURAL TRADITIONS

Luath Press Limited

committed to publishing well written books worth reading

LUATH PRESS takes its name from Robert Burns, whose little collie Luath (*Gael.*, swift or nimble) tripped up Jean Armour at a wedding and gave him the chance to speak to the woman who was to be his wife and the abiding love of his life. Burns called one of *The Twa Dogs* Luath after Cuchullin's hunting dog in *Ossian's Fingal*. Luath Press grew up in the heart of Burns country, and now resides a few steps up the road from Burns' first lodgings in Edinburgh's Royal Mile.

Luath offers you distinctive writing with a hint of unexpected pleasures.

Most UK and US bookshops either carry our books in stock or can order them for you. To order direct from us, please send a £sterling cheque, postal order, international money order or your credit card details (number, address of cardholder and expiry date) to us at the address below. Please add post and packing as follows: UK – £1.00 per delivery address; overseas surface mail – £2.50 per delivery address; overseas airmail – £3.50 for the first book to each delivery address, plus £1.00 for each additional book by airmail to the same address. If your order is a gift, we will happily enclose your card or message at no extra charge.

Luath Press Limited
543/2 Castlehill
The Royal Mile
Edinburgh EH1 2ND
Scotland
Telephone: 0131 225 4326 (24 hours)
Fax: 0131 225 4324
email: sales@luath.co.uk
Website: www.luath.co.uk

The Quest for the Wicker Man

History, folklore and Pagan perspectives